Overseas Investments, Capital Gains and the Balance of Payments

CLIFF PRATTEN

Department of Applied Economics,
University of Cambridge

Published by
INSTITUTE OF ECONOMIC AFFAIRS
1992

First published in February 1992 by

The Institute of Economic Affairs,
2 Lord North Street,
Westminster, London SW1P 3LB

Research Monograph 48

ISSN 0073-9103
ISBN 0-255 36303-6

*The Institute gratefully acknowledges financial support for its
publications programme and other work from a generous benefaction
by the late Alec and Beryl Warren.*

Printed in Great Britain by
Goron Pro-Print Co. Ltd.,
Churchill Industrial Estate, Lancing, W. Sussex
Filmset in 'Berthold' Univers 9 on 11pt Medium

Contents

Foreword

The concept of the nation state—stemming from tribalism, based on geography, fashioned by history—contains within it both strengths and weaknesses. The strength of cohesion and identity of purpose shows when a nation is under threat, as in time of war: its weakness shows when regional or global issues arise which circumscribe the nation state. As an island trading nation, Britain has shown its ability to make the most of its strengths over many centuries, but recently we seem to have been losing the international competitive war.

In this paper, the author takes official government statistics as his starting point and, using various methods, suggests that these statistics underestimate Britain's economic strength in relation to the investments made overseas through many generations. The difference between book value (used by government officials) and market value is so significant that we can be led to draw false conclusions by concentrating on the former.

It was during my time as Chief Executive of IBM United Kingdom (1965-85) that I became interested in balance-of-payments and balance-of-trade figures. It was my resolve that, taking one year with another, IBM would end up with a positive balance of trade. Certainly, over that 20-year period we were very much on the positive side because we were able to prove to IBM in Europe and America that the United Kingdom was a good place in which to invest and manufacture. There was continuous investment to the point that IBM United Kingdom rose to be among Britain's leading exporters. Indeed, in 1990 it was the country's fourth largest exporter. It is true that, because of the integrated nature of our operations, IBM United Kingdom was also a significant importer. Nevertheless, we did contribute positively to Britain's balance of trade.

Because it is reasonable to assume that any investment should receive a dividend, that capital injections should be serviced, it was not possible to have the same objective for the balance of payments as for the balance of trade. Even so, in some years when IBM United Kingdom exports were particularly strong, the company had a

9

positive impact on Britain's balance of payments since it had net receipts from the rest of the world.

During those years I attempted, with mixed success, to correlate my figures with official government statistics. As the author points out, the official statistics are often subject to considerable revision in an effort to make them more timely and accurate. It is strange that, even though we should know—and are indeed warned—that we must not judge on one month's figures alone, many people anxiously await the latest figures of surplus or deficit.

This paper examines the balance of payments, of which the balance of trade in goods is only a part. The contribution of services (such as banking, insurance and shipping) exemplified by the City of London, has ensured that the balance of Britain's trade in goods and services has been healthier than is often realised. But, as the author points out, capital gains on our overseas investments represent an additional (and generally ignored) contribution to our economic strength. For example, during the decade of the 1980s, capital gains of £82 billion were achieved—more than four times the current account deficit of the period.

Moreover, there has been another significant change relating to the quality of Britain's output. There is no doubt that, during the decade in question, there was a visible improvement in the reliability of delivery dates and the quality of products and service.

Since the end of the Second World War, Britain's share of world exports of manufactures declined from an unsustainably high 25 per cent to below 10 per cent. By the late 1980s, our share had apparently stabilised and indeed was showing signs of increasing as a result of continued investment in manufacturing industry and generally improved industrial performance. There is now increasing evidence that Japan's investment in Britain will, in due course, contribute positively to our balance of trade and to an improvement in our share of world trade.

The discovery of North Sea oil for a time masked the decline in Britain's manufacturing output, as is now recognised. But the nature of Britain's exports has also changed, reflecting the decline in heavy industries such as steel and shipbuilding, the demise of other industries such as motor cycles, and the move to knowledge-based industries such as pharmaceuticals and electronics. Although change has been painful, it has also emphasised our strengths. As a country we have limited raw materials. But our ability to innovate and add value, coupled with our financial system based on the City, mean that we are well placed to improve our position in world trade provided we make further progress in good marketing and management.

As the developed countries move towards serving the wants of more demanding consumers, manufacturing and service industries will inevitably move nearer the customer. Recognising the advantages of economies of scale, the cost of distribution systems and the increasing use of telecommunications, industrialists will feel the conflicting pressure of national sovereignty and commercial sense. Do we invest in manufacturing overseas? Or do we continue to export? There will be many answers according to industry and circumstances. However, while we continue to believe in the nation state—and recent events in Eastern Europe show that the concept is still alive—the ability to measure the effects of both outward and inward investment will be fundamental to our understanding of the increasingly complex world in which we live.

The need to measure our performance reliably is one reason I commend this paper which makes an important contribution to our understanding of Britain's balance of payments. The author has used the most up-to-date figures available to assess the evidence, using different methods to test and validate his conclusions. Even so, it is arguable he is attempting to define the contours of a lump of jelly on an oscillating platform.

The Institute of Economic Affairs is a research and educational charity. It urges its authors to follow their analysis to its conclusions, but it does not engage in advocacy. Its Directors, Advisers and Trustees must dissociate themselves from the arguments and conclusions of its authors. Nevertheless, we are indebted to Mr Pratten for the clarity of his conclusions and for his rigorous and intellectually honest approach to data which may sometimes be seen as unreliable.

January 1992   SIR EDWIN NIXON, CBE, DL

Sir Edwin Nixon, CBE, DL, is Deputy Chairman of National Westminster Bank PLC, Chairman of Amersham International plc, and a Director of Royal Insurance plc. He retired as Chairman of IBM United Kingdom Limited in May 1990 after 35 years' service, including 20 years as Chief Executive.

The Author

C. F. PRATTEN is Senior Research Officer, Department of Applied Economics, University of Cambridge, and a Fellow of Trinity Hall. He studied economics at Bristol University and is a Chartered Accountant. His first appointment in Cambridge was in 1960. After a spell at the National Economic Development Office when it was first set up he returned to Cambridge in 1963. His publications include studies of industrial structure: *The Economies of Scale in Manufacturing Industry*, Cambridge University Press, 1971; 'A Survey of the Economies of Scale', in *Studies on the Economics of Integration*, EC, 1988; and *The Competitiveness of Small Firms and the Economies of Scale*, CUP, 1990. In the 1970s he published two studies of labour productivity and industrial performance, *Labour Productivity within International Companies*, CUP, 1976; and *A Comparison of the Performance of Swedish and UK Companies*, CUP, 1976. His other publications include *Applied Macroeconomics*, 2nd Edition, Oxford University Press, 1990. He is presently working on a study of the stock market to be published in 1992.

Acknowledgements

Professor R. Eisner of Northwestern University, who pioneered new methods of valuing US direct investment, provided the share price data which was used for Section 6. Professor Eisner's help in providing these data was greatly appreciated. Participants at a seminar at the Faculty of Economics, two referees of a draft of the paper and Professor Geoffrey Wood made many constructive comments and provided insights which helped with the preparation of the final version of the paper.

C.P.

Introduction

During the post-1945 period the balance of payments has been an important influence on economic policy and yet one important element of the balance of payments, capital gains, has been little studied. This *Research Monograph* provides estimates of the capital gains Britain obtains on its net overseas assets and assesses the importance of the capital gains for the balance of payments. The current account balance, which is calculated in nominal terms and excludes capital gains and losses, is usually taken as providing the 'score' for the balance of payments: put simply, a deficit is taken as an indication that Britain is living beyond its means and a substantial current account deficit calls for deflation as a remedy. In practice, the balance-of-payments accounts are more complex—a current balance-of-payments deficit may be offset by capital gains and these are particularly important for the UK because of its large overseas equity investments which are partly financed by borrowing from overseas. Also, capital gains have increased in importance during the 1980s with the very rapid growth of international investment.

In this paper estimates are made of the market value of net direct investment overseas. (The main component of direct investment is the investment of companies in their subsidiaries operating in foreign countries.) In the past direct investment has been valued at book values; the valuation of direct investment at market values in this paper makes possible comprehensive estimates of capital gains on UK net overseas investments. Three methods are used to estimate the market value of net direct investment overseas, and all three methods indicate market values in excess of book values. The market value of net direct investment is estimated to have been £27 billion above the book value of £36 billion at the end of 1989. The conclusion of the paper is that Britain had substantial capital gains on its overseas investments during the 1980s and can expect capital gains in the future.

The paper is divided into three parts. The second part describes methods of estimating the value of Britain's direct investment overseas and direct investment in the UK by companies based overseas and reports the results of applying the methods. The first and third parts deal with capital gains on all types of assets and liabilities. Part 1 describes existing methods of measuring asset values for balance-of-payments purposes and estimates of Britain's balance-of-payments record using existing conventions. Part 3 provides revised estimates of the balance of payments including estimates of capital gains related to net direct investment, and an assessment of the importance and significance of capital gains.[1]

Throughout the paper data from the 1991 Pink Book, *United Kingdom Balance of Payments*, which provides statistics for 1990 and the preceding nine years, have been used as a basis for estimates. When the study reported in this paper was commenced, data for 1990 were not available and the focus of the work was the position at the end of 1989. During 1990 prices on world stock markets fell so market values of many investments were lower at the end of 1990 than they had been at the end of 1989. Early in 1991 prices on many stock markets recovered as the Iraq Gulf crisis was resolved, so the use of end-1990 valuations as a benchmark would be misleading. The effects of changes in valuations during 1990 and 1991 are considered in Section 9.

---

[1] The survey reported in this paper was financed by HM Treasury. The views expressed in the paper are personal and are not necessarily those of HM Treasury.

PART ONE:

Current Methods of Estimating Britain's Balance of Payments

chapter one

Current Methods of
Estimating Britain's
Balance of Payments

Theory and Practice

Income and Wealth

At the end of a year we may look back and compare our income from wages, dividends, etc., with our expenditure on goods and services. If our income exceeds our expenditure we have saved a part of our income and may conclude that we are better off at the year end. In fact, this could be misleading; if the value of our assets—house, shares, etc.—has fallen, we have sustained capital losses and we could be worse off in the sense that the value of our assets at the end of the year is less than at the beginning of the year. In practice, in most years the value of our assets rises at least in money terms, but to assess the change in our *net** wealth at the end of each year we should adjust the value of our net assets in money terms between the beginning and the end of the year for the change in the general level of prices during the year.

In spite of the importance of *capital gains** and losses, many people aim to keep their expenditure within their income and one reason for doing this is that the value of assets fluctuates from day to day. If we slavishly related our expenditure to our income minus any real capital losses or plus any real capital gains, our expenditure would have to vary with fluctuations in asset prices and this would certainly be inconvenient in the aftermath of a stock market crash or a fall in house prices. Over a longer time-span, people do take more account of capital gains and losses; they do not ignore changes in the value of their wealth. For example, by 1989 the boom in house prices during the 1980s was boosting consumers' expenditure and the decline in house prices since 1989 is now a constraint on the growth of consumers' spending.

This paper is not concerned with the income and wealth of individuals, but a similar dilemma faces the nation in its transactions with the rest of the world. These can be measured in terms of exports and imports of goods and services which result in a current account deficit or surplus or in terms of changes in the

---

*Words and phrases set in italics and followed by an asterisk are defined/explained in the 'Glossary', below, pp. 115-118.

UK's net overseas assets and liabilities—its external wealth which takes account of capital gains and losses as well as exports of goods and services.

Like the assets owned by individuals, the UK's overseas assets and liabilities fluctuate in value—and there is an added complication. Records of the overseas assets owned by UK residents are not comprehensive and the estimates are subject to substantial revision. An extreme example of the extent of these revisions is that the UK's total net external assets at the end of 1989 were estimated to be £112·5 billion in the 1990 Pink Book: a year later, the 1991 Pink Book estimate was £83·7 billion, a reduction of 26 per cent, and this change which also affects estimates of capital gains, the subject of this *Research Monograph*, was not caused by changes in the principles used to value assets but by additional data becoming available. This makes attempts to establish Britain's balance-of-payments position difficult; nevertheless, it is important to make the attempt.

The conventional focus on transactions in the balance-of-payments accounts and the frequent omission of any reference to stocks of assets and liabilities and capital gains imparts a gloomy bias to perceptions of Britain's balance of payments. During the 1980s capital gains on Britain's overseas investments more than offset the deficit on the *current account**. This was not a flash in the pan.

Balance-of-Payments Accounts

The purpose of the UK balance-of-payments accounts is to identify and record *transactions* between residents of the UK and non-residents 'in a way that is suitable for analysing the economic relationships between the UK economy and the rest of the world'.[1] The balance-of-payments accounts, like national income statistics, focus on transactions (income and *capital transactions**), and deal with statements of assets and liabilities (balance sheets) as an appendage to the main accounts. The concentration on transactions in part reflects the historic development of national income accounting and that data on transactions were more readily available than data for stocks.[2] Also, the valuation of assets and liabilities entails problems of principle which have not been fully resolved.

---

[1] The Pink Book 1990, p. 5.

[2] Stone (1964) notes that 'work on stocks . . . lagged behind work on flows and that balance sheet data is not at present available as an integral part of the national accounts' (p. 110).

The Published Accounts of Companies and the Balance-of-Payments Accounts

Published company accounts provide information which investors use when deciding in which firms to invest, while the balance-of-payments accounts provide information for investors deciding in which countries to invest (as well as influencing the decisions of macro-economic policy-makers), and this comparison is instructive for a number of reasons. Both sets of accounts provide a similar range of information—data on income flows, sources and applications of funds, and assets and liabilities. Both sets of accounts are prepared within a framework of conventions and an eclectic approach is used for valuing assets for inclusion in balance sheets—in both cases marketable securities are valued at market prices, while plant and machinery are usually valued in company accounts at historical cost less accumulated *depreciation**, and these data are used for valuing *direct investment** overseas and direct inward investment in the balance-of-payments accounts.

The conventions used to prepare company accounts have been subject to much recent comment. Two criticisms of existing methods are that they fail to adjust profits and asset values for the effects of inflation, thereby misrepresenting profits and asset values, and that they do not provide information about the state and prospects for companies which could be provided and which would enable investors to make better informed assessments of the prospects for companies. These criticisms of corporate accounts have parallels with the balance-of-payments accounts, which are not adjusted for inflation and for which the valuation of some assets could be misleading; in particular, direct investment overseas is not valued at current market values.

Responses to these criticisms are that users of accounts understand traditional accounting conventions such as *historical cost accounting**, that these conventions are efficient in use in the sense that the calculations required are straightforward and limited, that they involve the use of less judgement than current cost accounting, are less subjective and are less susceptible to *'creative accounting'**. *Earnings** per share estimated using the historical cost convention provide an indication of the value of a company's shares, and attempts to value assets at current values may add little information, especially if there is uncertainty about the basis of valuation of the assets. It is also relevant that the use of current cost accounting to supplement historical cost statements was abandoned by companies during the 1980s. Before leaving the comparison between company accounts and balance-of-payments accounts, one other contrast is remarked upon: the disposition of the assets and liabilities of a company are generally within the control of its directors—they can sell existing assets providing they can find a buyer and hold cash, etc.; in the case of Britain's balance of payments the assets and liabilities held by private agents are not controlled by the government.

Economic Relationships

One reason for re-assessing the information concerning the balance of payments to be collected from agents and published is changing perceptions of economic relationships. In part these changes are a response to changes in the economy which alter the relative importance of some relationships, and in part a response to changing economic theories developed to explain the operation of the economy. The relative importance of stocks of assets and liabilities compared to flows is a case in point. Keynesian macro-economic models of the economy which were developed in the 1950s and 1960s concentrated on income flows; stocks were acknowledged but they played a small part in these models. During the 1970s and 1980s monetarist models which made great play of the *stock* of and changes in the stock of money were fashionable. Both sets of models failed to forecast the extent *and timing* of the boom in 1987/88 and the recessions in 1980/81 and 1990/91.

Explanations for these failures include the difficulties of modelling the response of agents to shocks, and the fact that existing models do not fully incorporate the effects of the interactions between changes in the value of asset holdings and financial and income flows or the causes and effects of changes in expectations. During the 1980s, equity assets—shares and property—soared in value, partly in response to increasing profitability of companies and financial deregulation—a one-off change which freed the movement of capital between countries and lending within countries.

Particularly important changes for the economic relationships considered in this paper were the removal of controls on overseas investment by UK residents, and globalisation of financial markets. The Exchange Control Act of 1947 enabled the government to control overseas investment. The controls were abolished in October 1979. These changes led to a rapid build-up of overseas assets and liabilities; total external assets of UK residents increased by 358 per cent between the end of 1979 and the end of 1990, and *portfolio investment** in overseas securities increased by 1,367 per cent.

20

Capital transactions put through the foreign exchanges now dominate trade flows, and recent deficits on the current account, although large in relation to past deficits, are small relative to *gross** UK assets and liabilities. (The deficit in 1989, £20 billion, can be compared with estimated total UK external liabilities of £887 billion at the end of 1989. Equivalent figures for 1974, when the deficit reached an earlier peak, were a deficit of £3·4 billion and total external liabilities of £30·1 billion.)

Economic theorists have kept pace with the changing relative importance of stocks and asset markets and at varying levels of abstraction have developed models which incorporate asset markets, including equity asset markets and theories of asset price determination. Examples are Blanchard and Fischer (1989), Casson (1990) and Weale *et al.* (1989).

Wealth effects have long been recognised in the literature; the wealth of households influences consumers' expenditure and theories of investment behaviour have been built around the *valuation ratio**—the ratio of the market values of *equities** to the *book values**. Similarly, the market values of company shares influence existing and potential lenders and creditors and the opportunity for companies to raise fresh equity capital. Finally, changes in expectations lead to financial flows, as investors invest or withdraw investments, and cause changes in exchange rates (unless the authorities compensate for the changes in financial flows). In these ways rational expectations of future developments which influence share prices have an impact on current events.

During February 1991, newspapers reported that there had been a collapse of consumer and business confidence in the aftermath of the start of the Gulf War—there was a temporary buyers' strike. Most models do not incorporate confidence because it is hard to quantify. The perceived state of Britain's balance of payments, including its net overseas asset position, could affect confidence and hence many decisions involving the flow of funds to and from the UK, investment and, perhaps, consumers' expenditure. Confirmation that investors do take some account of the UK's net overseas assets is provided by comments in a broker's circular (Skeoch and Hacche, 1990):

'The UK's net asset position is not just something of academic interest but is in itself a very important indicator of the sustainability of the current account position at current levels of the exchange rate and interest rates.'

Published information about Britain's balance of payments could affect perceptions of the actual state of the balance of payments and hence economic decisions and so may have a direct effect on the operation of the economy.

The Balance-of-Payments Score

Cohen (1969) noted that

> 'any country would be well advised to employ a variety of [measures of the balance of payments] in order to derive the most complete picture of its balance of payments position. Most countries, though, seem to prefer a simple, clear and straightforward, if possibly misleading, definition' (p. 42).

As with other activities there is a requirement for a measure which encapsulates the state of the balance of payments. Winters (1985) has referred to one measure, the current account balance identity, as the 'fundamental equation of balance-of-payments theory'; it represents 'national net acquisition of foreign assets during a period' (pp. 166, 168). Many economists focus on the current account balance without qualification or explanation (for example, Dornbusch (1988), Krugman (1989)). An alternative measure of the state of Britain's balance of payments is the stock of net assets and changes in the stock which include capital gains. In practice, for the public the focus of attention is the current account balance which is published monthly—in crude terms a deficit indicates that Britain is living beyond its means and carries the threat that the economy will have to be deflated to eliminate the deficit. The implication of a current balance-of-payments deficit is that Britain's net overseas assets are falling; but this is not necessarily the case because of changes in the value of Britain's assets and liabilities— that is, capital gains (or losses).

The balance-of-payments score is important for another reason. As noted earlier, capital transaction flows through the exchanges greatly exceed income flows. There is a danger that if the balance-of-payments 'score' of a country is perceived to be unfavourable, capital flows will be influenced. For example, *if the current account balance for a country is in substantial deficit, that may lead to an expectation of a devaluation of its currency even though the deficit is covered by capital gains.*

The Weakness in Balance-of-Payments Accounts

This paper is concerned with two related problems involved in the measurement of the balance of payments—the measurement of income and the measurement of capital gains. The national income and balance-of-payments accounts measure flows at current prices, not income. Income has been defined as the amount of expenditure which an agent can sustain during a period but be equally well off at the end of the period as he was at the beginning (Hicks, 1939). If income is defined in *real**, not *nominal**, terms, then the income or current account would include adjustments for the effects of inflation on asset values and capital gains (or losses).

The practical flaw in this definition, which Hicks recognised, is that if it is used for periods as short as a year, the instability of asset prices and hence capital gains gives erratic estimates of income. One solution is to use the definition for an extended period; another possibility is to estimate the *trend* rate of growth of asset prices and total return on investments. In effect, normal or *'permanent' income** is substituted for actual income.

The second problem is linked to the first; again it involves changes in the value of assets and liabilities. At present an eclectic approach is used to value assets; while portfolio investments[1] are valued at market prices, direct investments are valued at book values. (Book values are the values of investments in the books of the companies owning the investments; book values of fixed assets are based on cost or subsequent *revaluation** less accumulated depreciation provisions.) In aggregate, these values of direct investments are acknowledged to be below the written down replacement cost of the assets and market values. The under-valuation which affects the estimates of capital gains occurs for three reasons *(or sources of errors)*:

(A) Inflation has raised the costs of replacing fixed assets. (This does not apply to assets and liabilities which are fixed in terms of money, but stocks, especially if valued on a *last-in-first-out** (LIFO) basis as they are by American companies, are affected. UK companies usually value stocks on a *first-in-first-out** (FIFO) basis and so most stocks are valued for balance-sheet purposes at near to current replacement cost.)

(B) On average, companies value assets on a conservative basis in part to limit future depreciation charges. For example, when companies make acquisitions they often write down the book value of the assets acquired and write-off the excess of the price they pay over the book value of the assets acquired.

---

[1] Portfolio investment covers all investment in securities with an original contractual maturity of more than one year, as well as in corporate equities, bonds and other securities with no specified maturity and which are not direct investments. Direct investments are investments, usually in companies, that are financially and organisationally related and are situated in different countries. A direct investment in a company means that the investor has a significant influence on the operations of the company.

(C) The book values of assets generally exclude goodwill and other intangible assets—put another way, for many companies the market values of their businesses exceed the book value of their assets, reflecting in a rough and ready way the value of intangible assets such as goodwill, the sunk costs of building-up businesses, etc.

There can be little doubt that at the end of 1989 direct investment was in some sense undervalued. This raises two questions. Does the method of valuation matter? What are the alternative methods of valuation?

Does the Basis of Valuation of Direct Overseas Investment Matter?

The reasons for attempting to make as accurate estimates as possible of the value of direct overseas investment—which means estimating hypothetical market values—are:

(a) to provide information for agents so that they can make better informed decisions;

(b) to model the economy more accurately;

(c) to provide policy-makers with a more comprehensive guide to the state of Britain's balance of payments which reflects the underlying state of affairs and happens to give a more optimistic view of Britain's dealings with the rest of the world than the current account balance taken in isolation.

In the USA the trigger for revaluation seems to have been the perception of the US as a net debtor and attempts to reverse that perception, rather than concern about the effects on decisions by agents and by economic modelling.

One argument for not using market values is that they are unstable; nevertheless the market prices are often the best estimates of value available. Also, the instability of share prices applies equally to portfolio investments which are valued at current market values, and the fluctuating values and instability affect the operation of the economy and so they should be incorporated in models. There are advantages to be obtained by assessing hypothetical market values for UK direct investment overseas and such estimates could have important implications for both government and private sector economic decisions.

The inconsistencies of the existing practices used for valuing direct investment are illustrated in Box 1, where the practices are applied to Glaxo.

Glaxo — An Illustration

Glaxo, a pharmaceutical company, provides an extreme example of the inconsistency of the present methods of valuing Britain's overseas net assets. Using existing conventions, Glaxo's overseas operations are included as direct investment at book value. The book value of its overseas assets may be of the order of £2 billion at June 1991. The current stock market value of Glaxo is £20 billion, and shareholders resident overseas own perhaps 30 per cent of the company's shares. These 'portfolio' holdings would be valued at market prices and shown as a liability of £6 billion in Britain's balance of assets and liabilities. Thus for official statistics the net valuation of Glaxo's overseas investment and the overseas holdings in the company is a liability of £4 billion. The argument of this paper is that it would be more consistent to value Glaxo's investment overseas in terms of the market price of its shares, say, 60 per cent of £20 billion, i.e. £12 billion, to give net assets of £6 billion instead of a net liability of £4 billion.

Between the end of 1989 and June 1991 the market value of Glaxo increased by approximately £8 billion. Using the present methodology for compiling official estimates of Britain's assets and liabilities, this would result in increased net liabilities of about £2 billion and have no effect on assets; using the revised method suggested in this paper, the effect would be an increase in Britain's net assets less liabilities of approximately £5 billion, equivalent to 36 per cent of the UK's current account deficit in 1990.[1]

---

[1] It is assumed for the purpose of these calculations that the proportion of Glaxo's shares owned by shareholders resident overseas did not change during the period from the end of 1989 to June 1991. In fact considerable changes take place in the proportion of shares held by persons resident overseas.

Methods of Valuing Direct Investment

Broadly, there are two methods of revaluing direct investment: either book value estimates can be revised to take account of inflation—stocks of fixed assets can be increased in line with price indices for acquisitions of fixed assets—or stock market values can

25

be used. The first method, the use of price indices for fixed assets (and stocks, if appropriate), adjusts in an approximate way for type 'A' errors, the effects of inflation on fixed asset values and follows the procedures used for the national income accounts, but it does not adjust for type 'B' and 'C' errors which are defined on pages 23 and 24. The second method, using market values, should correct for all three types of error.[1]

Estimates of the market values of direct investment are more *relevant* to the process of taking economic decisions than are historical cost estimates or estimates of replacement costs of the underlying tangible and monetary assets. Two developments which occurred during the 1980s have made the use of share valuations for making realistic valuations of direct investments practicable. Firstly, many UK companies have invested overseas to an extent where a half or more of their assets are overseas and so a major part of their share valuations relate to their overseas assets. Secondly, the internationalisation of stock markets has increased the credibility of stock market valuations. National stock markets are not as segmented because more investors are free to move funds between markets.

Another test of a method of valuation is the *reliability* of the estimates. One problem with valuing direct investment in terms of stock market values is that most direct investments are not in quoted shares. (There are exceptional cases: for example, where a UK company has a majority holding in a US or Australian company which is quoted.) An indication of market values—the prices at which holdings could be sold—has to be obtained in some other way. There are three methods of estimating the *hypothetical* 'market values' of direct investments.

First, if it is assumed that the values of *direct* investment overseas move in line with share prices in the countries in which the investments are made from the date the investments are made until the date of the valuation, share prices for similar companies in the

---

[1] In some American studies, indices of prices for investment goods, such as machinery, have been used to revalue total direct investment, not investment in fixed assets alone; one interpretation of these estimates is that the prices of all the assets acquired move in line with those for investment goods. An important qualification to this procedure is that some of the monetary gains associated with inflation are included as profits; depreciation charges are below those based upon replacement costs and, for UK companies, stock appreciation is included as profits. The use of price indices can therefore lead to double-counting. Also the price of assets denominated in money terms, cash and debtors, does not inflate in line with inflation. The qualifications are considered to be so fundamental that the method has not been used to revalue UK direct investment in this paper.

host country can be used to estimate these hypothetical market values. The Bank of England used this method whose application had been pioneered by American economists (Eisner and Pieper, 1988) for a preliminary study for which the results were outlined in the *Bank of England Quarterly Bulletin* (November 1990). It assumed that the value of direct investments in, say, the USA moved in line with an index of US equity prices.

Second, the market values of shares in the companies with direct investments overseas can be apportioned between the part of the value which relates to domestic and the part which relates to the overseas investments; one method of apportioning the market value of companies is in proportion to the profits earned from domestic and overseas operations. This is the method developed at the University of Cambridge Department of Applied Economics (henceforward referred to only as the DAE).

Third, an estimate of current market values can be made by assigning a capital value to the earnings derived from overseas investment. The multiplier used to gross up earnings could be based upon the relationship between stock market values of companies and earnings for domestic companies operating similar businesses in the host country.

Estimates of market values based on share prices move more erratically through time than values based on the use of price indices for fixed investments. However, these erratic movements of share prices probably reflect values at which businesses could be sold more faithfully than movements of price indices for new investment goods. The prices in the market for businesses are affected by the state of trade and expectations, which are also important influences on share prices.

A qualification to hypothetical market values is that most direct investments overseas are substantial *stakes** in businesses. Certainly, during the boom in financial markets in the 1980s, stakes were usually sold at a premium to stock market prices— companies were willing to pay a premium to get control of businesses. During a recession, as in 1990/91, the saleability of stakes is more problematic and, in some cases, the sale price per share for a substantial stake could be below the market price for small parcels of shares.

Another problem involved in the valuation of overseas investments at market values is that some direct investments (for example, *subsidiaries** which market and sell UK exports) form part of integrated businesses and the sale of these investments would reduce UK exports of goods and receipts of royalties and hence would reduce the value of these businesses.

27

TWO

Official Estimates of Britain's Balance of Payments Record During the 1980s

The Current Account in Perspective

Before examining and applying methods of revaluing direct investments overseas and inward direct investments, the official estimates of Britain's balance of payments and capital gains are summarised. The current account of the balance of payments on which attention is focussed is estimated in nominal terms and excludes capital gains and losses. Table 1 puts the current account balance during the 1980s in perspective. Britain's current account deficit of £17·2 billion is shown in row 2 of Table 1 (this is the aggregate deficit—in some years there was a surplus, but over the 10 years the deficits exceeded the surpluses by £17·2 billion). The current account deficit was greatly exceeded by the capital gains which were estimated in the official statistics at £62·2 billion (row 7 of the Table). The picture is muddied by the *balancing item**, £26·0 billion (shown in row 4), which reflects unrecorded transactions and errors in the recording of those transactions which are identified. If the unrecorded transactions reflected by the balancing item were, in fact, unrecorded exports, then that would reduce the deficit, but the unrecorded transactions are more likely to reflect unrecorded capital inflows.[1] If the balancing item is unrecorded capital inflows, it would reduce Britain's net external assets at the end of the period which are estimated at £83·7 billion. The estimates of capital gains are made by subtracting the investment flow for a period from the change in the value of assets between the beginning and end of the period.[2]

---

[1] Between publication of the 1990 and 1991 Pink Books the balancing item for the 1980s was reduced from £46·2 billion to £26 billion. Most of the newly discovered transactions reflected capital flows, not unrecorded exports.

[2] For example, between the end of 1979 and the end of 1989 net external assets increased from £12·4 billion to £83·7 billion = £71·3 billion (Table 1.2 of Pink Book 1991). During the 1980s the net capital transactions outflow was £9·2 billion (Table 1.4), indicating capital gains of £62·2 billion.

Table 1:
Britain's Balance of Payments during the 1980s
(As recorded in the Balance of Payments Pink Book 1990)

(a) *In nominal terms*	£bn.	Year	As percentage of: GDP	Export of goods
Net external assets at the end of 1979	+12·4	1980	5·3	26·3
Less the current account deficit during the 1980s	−17·2	1985	−4·8	22·1
	−4·8			
Add the balancing item during the 1980s	+26·0	1985	7·3	33·3
Add allocation of SDRs	+0·3			
	+21·5			
Add capital gains during the 1980s	+62·2	1985	17·5	79·8
Net external assets at the end of 1989	+83·7	1989	16·3	90·6
(Net assets at the end of 1989 at end of 1979 prices)[a]	+42·8			

(b) *In real terms*	£bn. at end-1979 prices	As percentage of GDP in 1980
Net external assets at the end of 1979	+12·4	5·3
Net overseas investment	+11·4	4·9
Capital gains	+19·1	8·2
Net external assets at the end of 1989	+42·8[b]	18·5[b]

[a] The retail price indices for December 1979 and December 1989 were used to convert values at the end of 1989 to end-1979 prices.

[b] The difference between the sum of the items and the total is attributable to rounding.

Capital Gains

The current account balance is a balance between large flows; if the balance is small relative to the flows, the fact that capital gains are much larger than the balance may not be of much significance. To deal with this problem of comparison, the components of the balance of payments in part (a) of Table 1 are related to GDP and

Table 2:
Capital Gains during the 1980s

(At current prices)

		Type of Investment			
	Total	Direct	Portfolio	Other Assets	(Ordinary Shares)[1]
			£ billion		
Net external assets end of 1979	+12·4	+9·4	+2·3	+0·7	(+5·0)
Net overseas investment 1980-1989	+9·2	+50·3	+31·0	−72·1	(+3·9)
Capital gains	+62·1	−23·5	+78·1	+7·5	(+72·7)
Net external assets at the end of 1989	+83·7	+36·2	+111·4	−63·9	(+81·6)

[1] Included in portfolio investment.

exports of goods. The total capital gains in nominal terms during the 1980s represented 17·5 per cent of GDP in 1985 and 79·8 per cent of exports of goods in that year. Nominal capital gains are calculated without allowing for (deducting) the erosion of the value of assets valued in nominal terms caused by inflation.

Section (b) of Table 1 summarises the balance of payments in *real* terms. The current account balance, the allocation of *SDRs** (Special Drawing Rights), and the balancing item shown in the first part of the Table, sum to net overseas investment shown in the second part. (During the 1980s the current account deficit was − £17·2 billion, the allocation of SDRs + £0·3 billion, and the balancing item + £26·0 billion: net investment was therefore £9·2 billion at current prices.) The real capital gains at end-1979 prices, £19·1 billion, are smaller than the capital gains at current prices, £62·2 billion, reflecting the impact of inflation post-1979 to inflate the value of the UK's net overseas assets measured at current prices.

Table 2 analyses net external assets, investment and capital gains between direct, portfolio and other assets which are made up of loans to overseas residents by UK banks and other UK residents, borrowing from overseas residents by UK banks and other UK residents, the official reserves and other external assets and liabilities of the government. Since 1979, there has been a mushroom-like growth of portfolio investment overseas as UK investors have taken advantage of the freedom to invest overseas, but the largest part of the growth has been from capital gains. The capital gains on portfolio investment were £78·1 billion compared to total capital gains of £62·1 billion, and most of the capital gains on portfolio investment were on investments in *ordinary shares**, £72·7 billion, shown in the final column of Table 2. These gains reflect:

(a) increases in prices of shares which in turn in part reflect expected earnings on *ploughed-back profits**;

(b) devaluation—when sterling falls relative to the US dollar, the sterling value of assets denominated in dollars rises.

According to the official estimates, net direct investment of £9·4 billion represented 76 per cent of total net assets of £12·4 billion at the end of 1979 (row 1 of Table 2) and, during the 1980s, net direct investment was £50·3 billion, more than total net investment of £9·2 billion (row 2), but there were capital losses on direct investment of £23·5 billion during the 1980s (row 3).

The capital losses and absence of capital gains on direct investment are noteworthy. There are three explanations:

(i) Ploughed-back profits on direct investments are treated as new investment. (This contrasts with the treatment of ploughed-back profits related to portfolio investment which are not included as income or new investment.) The differences in the treatment of ploughed-back profits does not explain the absence of capital gains on direct investment. During the 1980s net ploughed-back profits (the unremitted profits of overseas subsidiaries) were £24 billion. So leaving aside ploughed-back profits, net assets at book value at the beginning of the 1980s were £9·4 billion and there was net investment of £26·3 billion apart from ploughed-back profits, a total of £35·7 billion, and yet net direct investment at the end of 1989 was valued at only £36·2 billion.

(ii) Direct investment is valued at book values. As noted in Section 1, replacement values generally exceed book values.

(iii) Revaluations, including revaluations attributable to changes in exchange rates, and write-offs are included as capital losses as they lower book values. Write-offs are not shown separately in the official statistics but the CSO reported that between the end of 1984 and the end of 1987 write-offs on UK direct investment overseas amounted to nearly £10 billion (*The*

31

Table 3:
Income from Overseas Investments in 1989

	Total	Direct	Portfolio	Other
Average net external assets in 1989[1] (£bn.)	82·3	34·5	91·4	−43·5
Net income from net assets in 1989 (£bn.)	4·1	7·8	1·2	−4·9
Income yield (per cent)	5·0	22·6	1·3	11·3

[1] Average of estimated holdings at the beginning and end of the year.

Census Report (*Business Monitor*, MO4, 1987)). The Report states that the write-offs include most notably the writing off directly to reserves of intangibles such as goodwill following the completion of acquisitions, and the writing down of the value of existing assets as a result of business and economic changes. The Report also states that the level of liabilities in respect of inward investment was less affected by revaluations and that write-offs of intangibles following acquisitions of UK companies were relatively insignificant.

The valuation of direct investment is the subject of Part 2 of this *Research Monograph*. This will show that, in terms of market values, direct investment is under-estimated and that that has led to an under-estimation of capital gains. The undervaluation of direct investment is supported by the estimates of yields shown in Table 3; the income yield on direct investment as valued in the official statistics in 1989 was 22·6 per cent.

Another noteworthy feature of the analysis shown in Table 2 is the capital gains on 'other assets', £7·5 billion (column 4, row 3), and of £5·4 billion on portfolio investment not in ordinary shares (column 3, row 3, *minus* column 5, row 3). One explanation for these gains is the devaluation of sterling. (Bonds, included in portfolio investment, and loans denominated in a foreign currency owned by UK investors, included in other assets, appreciate in sterling terms when sterling is devalued.) Also bond prices can rise or fall resulting in capital gains or losses. As 'other assets' (column 4 of Table 2) have changed, from £0·7 billion at the end of 1979 to liabilities of −£63·9 billion at the end of 1989, as a result of borrowing to offset Britain's current account deficit and overseas investment, any gains or losses on these liabilities could now be important because the amounts involved are much larger.

Income from Overseas Investment

The income yield on net portfolio investment shown in column 3, row 3 of Table 3 is significant. In 1989 the UK earned only £1·2 billion on its net portfolio investment of £91·4 billion.[1] One explanation for the low income yield was that a higher proportion of outward portfolio investment was invested in ordinary shares and a smaller proportion in bonds than for inward investment. Bonds have a higher income yield than ordinary shares but the latter show greater capital appreciation, which is not included in income.

Perusal of the UK balance-of-payments statistics indicates a strong *prima facie* case that net UK direct investment overseas is undervalued. Official statistics suggest that the UK sustained a loss of £23·5 billion on its net direct investment during the 1980s—and that is implausible. The high, 22·6 per cent, income return on net direct investment in 1989 also points to an undervaluation and hence an under-estimate of capital gains on net direct investment during the 1980s.

---

[1] There are qualifications to the data because estimates of some of the components of income are made by statisticians without access to information about income flows.

PART TWO

The Valuation of Direct Investment

THREE

Previous Estimates of the Value of UK Direct Investment

The Estimates

Table 4 summarises previous estimates of UK direct overseas investment valued at book values and at estimated market prices. The methods of valuing overseas investments at market prices were described on pages 25-27.[1]

The first point to note about the estimates in Table 4 is that the three estimates of net assets at the end of 1989 are substantially different. The CSO 'book value' estimate of net direct investment at the end of 1989 reported by the Bank of England in November 1990 was £58·6 billion. The Bank of England's estimates of market values based on the use of *stock market indices** for the host countries suggest that revaluation at market values may reduce the *net* value of direct investment overseas; one explanation for this result is that during the 1980s UK stock market prices rose more rapidly than those in the host countries to Britain's overseas investment, especially the USA where about 40 per cent of UK direct investment measured at book value is located.[2] The Bank's estimates were based on a preliminary exercise, and it acknowledged that the direction of the correction to convert book values to hypothetical market values was 'far from clear'.

The DAE estimates, which were based on the apportionment of UK stock market values, suggested that market values for UK direct investment overseas were about twice book values. Estimates of market values for inward investment were not made, but if the same multiple had been used as for overseas investment, the effect would have been to double the value of net UK direct investment overseas.

---

[1] Estimates of net direct investment overseas revalued at current replacement cost for fixed assets are not available for the UK as they are for the USA. Unlike US statistics, the data collected from UK companies do not distinguish investment in different types of fixed assets, intangible assets, property, plant and machinery, etc., which could be used as a basis for revaluing fixed assets.

[2] CSO (1990), *Business Monitor*, MO4, p. 2.

Table 4:
Estimates of the Value of UK Direct Investment Overseas

Sources:	Valuation:	Assets	Liabilities £ billion	Balance
CSO	at book value, end-1989[a, b]	145·1	86·5	+58·6
Bank of England	at stock market prices of host countries, end-1988[a]			'may be' <58·6[c]
DAE	at domestic stock market prices (17.5.1990)[d]	290·2	(173·0)[e]	117·2

Notes:

[a] *Bank of England Quarterly Bulletin*, November 1990, p. 490.

[b] Based on the cost of assets when purchased or when last revalued.

[c] The Bank stated that its preliminary study using stock market prices to value UK direct investment 'yields the result that the "true" net asset position may be *less* (than the balance based on book values)'. The £58·6bn. is the CSO's figure shown in the first row of the Table.

[d] Estimates reported in 'Why Sterling has to go', *Financial Times*, 18 July 1990.

[e] It was *assumed* that the ratio of market value to book value was the same for inward as for outward investment, i.e. 2·0.

Qualifications
Bank of England Estimates
The qualifications to the Bank of England's estimates are described in Section 6 and are therefore only outlined here. An important reason for qualifying the estimates made by the Bank of England in its preliminary study is that the value of overseas and inward investments may not move in step with stock market indices.

Firstly, many direct investments overseas and inward investments, especially those made in recent years, were in the form of take-overs generally made at a premium to market values. This suggests that the market valuation should start at a discount to the cost; however, a contrary argument is that if and when a sale of such stakes is considered, a premium over stock market values may be obtained. Share values fluctuate and during the 1980s share prices rose very rapidly (at an average annual rate of 15 per cent), implying that share prices at the end of the 1970s were undervalued in relation to future dividends. Greenfield investments made in the UK during the 1970s would not be subject to this undervaluation and would not increase in value in line with equities.

38

An important qualification to the estimates if share price indices, such as the FT-Actuaries for the UK or Standard and Poor's for the USA, are used to estimate the values of direct investments is that there is an element of double-counting. One explanation for increases in share prices is *ploughed-back profits** which enhance future profits; if the stock of investment is revalued in line with stock market prices there is double-counting because in the official statistics ploughed-back profits are included as income on direct investment *and* as new investment. A further reason for qualifying the estimates is that the industrial pattern of UK overseas investment in host countries was different to the weighting of shares for those countries' share price indices which were used for the Bank of England's estimates. The distribution of both outward and inward investment is uneven in the sense that it is heavily concentrated—outward investment in the oil, food, drink and tobacco, chemicals (including pharmaceuticals), financial services and other services sectors; inward investment in the oil, chemicals, engineering, food, drink and tobacco, motor vehicle, and financial services industries. Oil companies accounted for about a quarter of the stock, measured at book value, of both outward and inward investment in 1987 (CSO (1990), *Business Monitor*, MO4, p. 9), compared with 11 per cent of the capitalisation of the FT-Actuaries All Share Index at the end of 1988.[1] The differences in weighting could be significant because movements of share prices for different sectors do vary. The use of stock market indices for valuing UK direct investment is less satisfactory than for US foreign investment because UK overseas investment is not so broadly spread across industries as US foreign investment.

Another qualification to the Bank of England's estimates which was acknowledged by the Bank is that UK share price indices which are used to value *inward* investment reflect the earnings of the overseas operations of UK companies as well as their domestic UK operations. These overseas operations make an important contribution to the prices of UK shares, but ideally these effects should be excluded when assessing the market value of *inward* investment in the UK. The same qualification applies to the use of stock market

---

[1] The weighting of direct investment overseas can be compared to the weighting for the output of the economy or stock market capitalisation. Here, the important comparison is with stock market capitalisation which affects stock market indices and as, for example, some food, drink and tobacco sector and pharmaceutical sector shares are highly valued by the stock market relative to book values, and these are overseas investment intensive sectors, the differences in weighting are dampened.

prices in other countries to value UK overseas investment; for example, the price of US shares is affected by profits of the companies which are expected to be earned in countries apart from the USA. Another drawback to the method is that the estimates are hypothetical in the sense that the values of investments in individual companies are not identified and cannot be assessed.

DAE estimates

The DAE method of estimating market values and the qualifications to estimates made by the method are described in detail in Sections 4 and 5, where the method is used to estimate the market value of overseas and inward investment, and in Appendix A. Qualifications to the original DAE estimates were that the estimate of market value for outward investment was based on a sample not a census and inward investment was not covered at all—it was *assumed* that the ratio of market value to book value was the same as for outward investment. Also, by implication, it was assumed that the overseas and domestic profits for each company were capitalised by the same multiples of profits before interest and tax. The extent of overseas and domestic borrowing and the division of taxes may vary from that for profits before interest and tax and affect the market's assessment of the value of overseas and domestic profits.

An essential difference between the American method which was used by the Bank of England and DAE methods is that different stock market prices are used to value direct investment. For the former, share prices in the country which is host to the investments are used and for the DAE method share prices in the country of domicile of the companies making the investments are used to value investments. For UK direct investments overseas the DAE method is particularly apt because a large share of profits of many UK companies is earned overseas and these profits influence and in some cases dominate the companies' share prices.

More generally, the applicability of the two methods turns on the reasons for differences in profitability and hence the value of assets—whether these are determined by differences in management and knowledge or by the location of assets. If the former applies, then the DAE method is appropriate; if the latter, the American method would be the right one to use. The point can be illustrated with an example. Is the value of IBM's Japanese subsidiary a reflection of IBM's management skills and knowledge which enable it to make profits in Japan or the fact that the subsidiary is sited in Japan and that any computer company in Japan is profitable and highly valued? In practice, both factors,

Table 5:
Reddaway's Estimates[a]

Valuation:	End-1955	End-1964
	£ million	
Book value	885·6	1,622·9
Market value	1,060·4	2,175·7
Ratio of market value to book value	1·20	1·34

[a] Reddaway (1968), p. 362. The estimates are for manufacturing, mining and plantations and exclude oil companies whose overseas investments were of a similar order of magnitude to those of the sample of companies included in manufacturing, etc.

management and location, affect profits, but the contribution of management and knowledge is probably the more important.

There are flaws in every method of estimating the market value of direct investment. In this paper several methods are used and the results are compared.

Historical Estimates of Direct Investment at Market Values

The only historical estimates of market values of direct investment overseas for the UK were made by Reddaway (1968). Reddaway's estimates shown in Table 5 were based on the actual stock market values of overseas investments for investments in companies (usually subsidiary companies) whose shares were quoted on an overseas stock market. (For the shares of a company to be quoted there have to be independent shareholders.) Estimates of the value of UK companies' interests in 'unquoted subsidiaries' were made 'as if they had been quoted' by managers of the firms completing Reddaway's questionnaires. The managers were asked to estimate what the value of the investments in their overseas subsidiary companies which were not quoted would be if the shares of the subsidiary companies were quoted. Where firms operated branches overseas they were asked 'to value their interest in the net assets of their overseas branches as if they had been turned into quoted companies'. Net amounts due from the subsidiaries to their parents on loan or credit accounts of all kinds were added to the actual or hypothetical market value of shares to relate to the book values of the parents' stakes in their subsidiaries. (The book values also included net loans and other borrowings.) A qualification to

Table 6:
Stock of Direct Investment at Book Value, 1968-90

	Direct Investment Overseas £bn.	Stock of: Inward Direct Investment £bn.	Net Direct Investment £bn.	As per cent of UK GDP at market prices %
1968	6·0	2·7	3·3	7·5
1970	6·8	3·3	3·5	6·8
1975	12·0	7·0	5·0	4·7
1980	33·2	26·4	6·8	2·9
1985	70·1	43·3	26·7	7·5
1989	129·4	93·3	36·2	7·1
1990	126·9	106·6	20·3	3·7

Source: The Pink Book 1991 and earlier issues.

Reddaway's estimates is that the important oil companies did not provide information for this part of the survey and were therefore excluded from his sample used to estimate market values.

Although official statistics do not record any capital gains on direct investment overseas, capital gains on direct investment were acknowledged by Reddaway. His estimates showed that between the end of 1955 and the end of 1964 the ratio of stock market values to book values had increased from 1·2 to 1·34.[1] To estimate an overall return on overseas investment, Reddaway combined the estimated capital gains and the after-tax profits for his sample; capital gains based on actual and hypothetical share values over the period 1955 to 1964 accounted for 28 per cent of the total return.

The Stock of Direct Investment at Book Values

Table 6 shows direct investment at book value. In relation to GDP, *net* direct investment overseas *at book value* fell between 1968 and 1980, then recovered but fell again (see final column of Table 6).

In 1985 only the USA had larger *gross* direct investments abroad

---

[1] Reddaway also obtained estimates of the replacement cost of fixed assets and these showed an increase over the book values of the assets of 15 per cent at the end of 1955 and 26 per cent at the end of 1964.

(before deducting inward investment) than the UK. UK direct investments were 40 per cent of those of the USA and about twice those of Japan, Germany, Switzerland and the Netherlands, the countries which had the next largest direct investments measured at book values.[1] (Japan's direct investments abroad have increased rapidly since 1985.) It has been estimated that the UK accounts for half of the total flow of direct investment from the EEC to countries outside the EEC, and about one-third of the flow of inward investment from outside the Community has been located in the UK.[2]

---

[1] *Source*: United Nations Centre for Transnational Corporations (1988), p. 25.
[2] Christine Spanneut (1990), pp. 28 and 29.

FOUR

Estimates of the Market Value of Direct Investment Overseas Using the DAE Method

The DAE method of estimating the value of direct investment overseas is to apportion the market value of a company between its domestic and overseas businesses according to the ratio of its profits or sales in those areas. The market value of a company is the valuation of the company's share capital on the stock market, the sum of its share capital at market prices on a selected day. The breakdown of profits or sales used to apportion the market value is that given by companies in their published annual reports and accounts. The principles used to apportion stock market values are straight-forward but there are difficulties of application relating to the definition of profits. Here we are concerned with the results of the exercise; the details of the methodology are described in Appendix A.

The Sample

Data for 140 companies were analysed for this study. Initially, the sample was taken from the largest UK-based companies in 'The Times 1,000' for 1988-89 (for which companies are ranked in order of turnover). Some large companies with no, or very few, overseas operations were excluded and were replaced by smaller companies with large overseas investments. (Fifty-six of the companies for which accounts were analysed were included among the largest 100 companies in *The Times*'s list which includes firms owned by companies based overseas and excludes property and insurance companies and banks, and 47 were among the next 150 companies listed.)

For 108 of the 140 companies, a profits breakdown between UK and overseas operations was available and was used to apportion the stock market values. For 28 of the remaining companies sales were used as a basis for apportionment, for two property companies rents were used, for Shell the value of net assets employed, and for Glaxo employment in the UK and overseas because the company does not publish a regional analysis of profits. (A regional analysis of profits relating to pharmaceutical discoveries would be difficult.)

For 53 of the 108 firms for which an analysis of profits was used to apportion share values, profits earned by overseas operations accounted for 50 per cent or more of total profits. Plainly the share values of many of the sample of companies are not dominated by their UK operations.

Book Value of Capital

As the measurement of the book value of the net assets employed at overseas subsidiaries is a topic which recurs in this paper, it is the subject of a separate box (Box 2, pp. 46-47).

Results

Share prices quoted in the *Financial Times* on 17 May 1990 were used to value the companies, and data from the latest published accounts for companies were used to apportion the market value between domestic and overseas operations. Prices on 17 May 1990 were used because that was the date on which the first estimates were made. Coincidentally, by the second half of May, companies whose accounting years end in December (the principal company reporting date and the reporting date for half of the sample of 140 companies) had published their results and this news was incorporated in their share prices—that is to say, share prices on 17 May 1990 took account of the information published in the accounts of many of the companies used for the analysis. The FT-Actuaries 500 Share index was 9·1 per cent lower on 17 May 1990 than on 31 December 1989, the date to which many of the estimates of the value of investments given in this paper relate—the substitution of share prices on 31 December 1989 for 17 May 1990 would *increase* the value of overseas investment.

The results are summarised in Table 7 (page 48). The market value of the overseas investments of the 140 companies based on apportionments of the total market values of the companies was £141·3 billion. When the book value of the equity of the companies was apportioned in the same way as market values, the total book value was £66·9 billion, slightly under half the market value. Market values exceeded estimated book values by £74·4 billion. This important result can be put another way. *The weighted average valuation ratio (of the market value of net assets to the book value of net assets) for the companies with overseas investments was just over two.*

The industrial analysis shown in Table 7 should be treated with

Book Values of Net Assets Employed at Companies' Overseas Operations

For the official estimates of direct investment, information about the book values of overseas investments is collected from companies. Book values of direct investment are defined as

> *'the sum of [companies'] investment in the ordinary and preference shares, loan and working capital and other capital funds and reserves of their overseas affiliates; less certain funds raised by overseas affiliates through the issue of loan stocks and subsequently redeposited with their UK parents'.*

There are two main components of the book value of companies' interests or stakes in their subsidiary or associate companies:

1. The book value of the parent company's stake in the capital of the subsidiary or associate. (Where, as is usually the case, the parent company owns all of the share capital of a subsidiary, its stake is the share capital of the subsidiary plus any reserves. Where a company does not own all of the share capital, then the proportion of the capital and reserves attributable to it depends upon its holding of the share capital.)

caution. Companies with interests in a number of industries were each allocated to a single industry, so the figures for food, drink and tobacco are inflated by the inclusion of BAT, which has subsidiaries operating in the financial services sector, and Unilever, which has subsidiaries in the chemicals and allied trades. Also, some of the overseas operations of companies assigned to sectors other than services, distribute products. The use of stock market prices to measure direct overseas investment increases the importance of the pharmaceuticals, services and food, drink and tobacco sectors because the ratio of stock market values to book values for these industries is high, reflecting the high level of profits relative to assets.[1]

---

[1] Weights based on the Census estimates of direct investment by industry were used to test the effects of the distribution of the sample companies among industries, but the weighted average ratio of market to book values was very close to the ratio for the total of all the companies given in Table 7.

2. Net loans to the subsidiary or associate from the parent company and net amounts due from the subsidiary. (The latter include normal trade credit for goods and services supplied to and bought from a subsidiary by other group companies.)

Companies have some flexibility for financing their subsidiaries and the choices are influenced by the profitability of subsidiaries' operations, tax considerations and the extent of trade between subsidiaries and other members of their groups. (If in the past a subsidiary has been profitable it may be largely financed by ploughed-back profits which are included in reserves.) Another factor which affects the proportions of stakes which are capital and accounts outstanding is the extent of write-offs. After acquisitions, many companies write-down the book values of the assets they acquire out of reserves and this reduces the book value of their stakes in the acquired companies' reserves, but not the net accounts outstanding due to parent companies which therefore increase as a proportion of total stakes.

Ideally, normal net trade credit would be excluded from the book value of companies' stakes in their subsidiaries when measuring the capital employed by subsidiaries for purposes of considering returns on investments. In practice it is not possible to separate normal trade credit from other outstanding accounts owed to parent companies.

Table 8 (page 49) lists the 12 companies with the largest overseas investments: these companies' overseas investments were more than half the total. For some of the 12 companies it was unusually difficult to estimate the value of overseas investment.

The treatment of the Anglo-Dutch companies, Royal Dutch-Shell and Unilever, is particularly important. For this exercise 40 per cent of the combined market value of the parent companies less 40 per cent of the share of the companies' investments which are in the UK are treated as overseas investment—that is, an estimate is made of the UK companies' share of the overseas investment of the companies. The treatment of the overseas investment of these companies for the official statistics of overseas investment is much more complex. For Unilever, UK overseas investment includes

o   Unilever Plc's overseas investment;

47

Table 7:
Value of Overseas Investments (excluding Banks),
at 17.5.1990

	Number of Companies	Estimated Market Value	Estimated Book Value	Ratio of Estimated Market Value to Estimated Book Value
		(£ billion)		
Chemicals	8	8·1	4·7	1·7
Pharmaceuticals	5	16·4	2·4	6·8
Engineering including electronics and vehicle components	27	10·3	4·9	2·1
Food, drink and tobacco	18	30·4	13·3	2·3
Building materials and construction	20	5·9	4·0	1·5
Oil	5	27·4	19·3	1·4
Services	23	14·5	4·2	3·5
Insurance companies	3	3·4	2·9	1·2
Other – mainly mining and other manufacturing	31	24·9	11·2	2·2
	140	141·3	66·9	2·1

o   Unilever's 40 per cent share of Unilever NV.

UK inward investment includes Unilever NV's 60 per cent share of Unilever Plc. For the Royal Dutch-Shell group the holdings of the two public companies in three holding companies, Shell Petroleum NV, The Shell Petroleum Co. Ltd., and Shell Petroleum Inc., are traced and this leads to contra holdings which exaggerate both outward and inward investment.

Coverage of Overseas Investment

According to the Pink Book 1991, direct overseas investment by industrial and commercial companies (including oil and insurance companies, but excluding banks and persons) had a book value of £118·4 billion at the end of 1989.[1] The CSO has estimated that the 100 companies with the largest overseas investments

---

[1] The component attributable to persons was estimated.

Table 8:
Companies with the Largest Overseas Investments

	Overseas Investments			
	Share of Profits Earned Overseas	Estimated Market Value £m	Estimated Book Value £m	Ratio of Estimated Market Value to Estimated Book Value
1. BP	74	12,800	7,981	
2. Shell	80[1]	12,070	9,587	
3. BAT	80	8,438	3,746	
4. Glaxo	60[2]	7,010	1,375	
5. Beecham	88	6,036	−261	
6. RTZ	96	5,129	2,475	
7. BTR	69	4,882	1,102	
8. ICI	59	4,680	2,958	
9. Cable & Wireless	90	4,654	1,199	
10. Guiness	82	4,646	2,402	
11. Unilever	80	4,247	1,019	
12. Hanson	44	3,979	478	
13. Reuters	82[3]	3,955	335	
		82,526	34,396	2·4

[1] Apportionment based on asset value.   [3] Apportionment based on sales.
[2] Apportionment based on employment.

accounted for 75 per cent of the total in 1989, or £88·8 billion. (Banks were excluded for the purpose of making the CSO's estimate, but oil and insurance companies were included.) The *estimated* book value of the overseas investments of the sample of 140 companies based on the apportionment of book values was £66·9 billion—57 per cent of the total figure.

Explanations for this difference are:

o The treatment of Shell and Unilever accounts for a part of the difference—the contra treatment boosts both outward and inward investment as recorded in the official statistics and this treatment is not limited to the two Anglo-Dutch companies.

49

Some of the UK subsidiaries of other overseas-based companies have operations overseas.

o Although the sample includes most of the public companies with large overseas investments, nearly 2,000 quoted companies with overseas investments are not included in the sample. (Assessing the scale of the overseas investment by smaller companies is complicated by the tendency for smaller firms to provide fewer analyses of the sources of profits in their published accounts. Smaller companies with overseas operations often give an analysis of turnover but not an analysis of profits by location of activity.)

o Unquoted companies are omitted from the exercise.

An obvious additional explanation for the difference between the £118·4 billion and the £66·9 billion is that the *actual* book values of stakes as recorded in official statistics are higher than the *estimated* book values of stakes. The inclusion of net amounts owed to parent companies, including amounts outstanding for goods and services supplied, in the official figures for stakes would have the effect of boosting the official measure of stakes, but write-offs after acquisitions might have the opposite effect *if* not all write-offs are put through the accounts of subsidiaries. (See Box 2 on pp. 46-47.) (If balances on inter-company accounts are included in companies' stakes in their subsidiaries, they have to be added to the market value of investments, as well as the book value of investments, to calculate the valuation ratio.)

The book value of home and overseas equity assets has been estimated from the analysis of profitability. There are three clues that these estimates may provide a realistic order of magnitude for the book value of assets overseas.

(1) For the sample of companies the weighted share of overseas profits and hence the estimated book value of the overseas assets represented 53 per cent of the total book value of equity assets. It is not a case of a small proportion of assets being located overseas; if the assets located overseas were a small percentage of total assets, the method used could lead to unreliable estimates.

(2) Seven companies besides ICI provided a geographic breakdown of overseas assets as well as profits. For these eight companies the average percentage of assets held overseas was 59 per cent, the *same* percentage as for profits.

(3) A comparison was made of the ratio of estimated total assets of the overseas operations to the estimated stakes in the overseas operations owned by the sample of companies from which the CSO obtained statistics. The results of the comparison are reported in Appendix A. The ratios were not inconsistent.

Summary

It has been shown that UK direct investment overseas valued at market prices on 17 May 1990 was substantially above book values. The conventional method of valuation in the official balance-of-payments statistics under-estimates the value of direct investment overseas. It is not possible to be as categorical about the extent of the difference between market and book values, but this is examined in Section 7 after other evidence has been reported.

FIVE

The DAE Method of Estimating the Market Value of Direct Investment Applied to Inward Investment

In principle the same method of valuing direct investment which was applied to UK overseas investment in Section 4 can be applied to inward investment. In this section inward investment is valued in terms of the share values of the companies which invest in the UK. For overseas investment, data published in the annual reports and accounts of UK companies were used to apportion market values between domestic UK and overseas operations. Companies based overseas do not state the proportion of their profits earned in the UK in their published annual reports and accounts, but it is possible to obtain this information for many companies from the published accounts of the UK subsidiaries of the companies.

The Sample

The initial sample of overseas companies with investments in the UK was obtained from the same source as for outward investment, that is, 'The Times 1,000', and this sample was supplemented by companies which were based overseas and which were known to have substantial UK operations. The companies were asked to provide the latest published annual accounts for their UK operations and for their parent companies. This section is based on an analysis of accounts for the UK operations of 75 companies which employed 390,000 people in 1989.[1] The 75 companies form only 2 per cent of all the overseas-based companies with investments in the UK. The domicile of the 75 companies, of which 39 were based in the USA, is shown in Table 9.

---

[1] Most, but not all, of the employees of the UK subsidiaries of overseas parent companies were located in the UK. Twelve of the companies for which accounts were analysed were included among the largest 100 companies in *The Times*'s list and 22 were included in the next 150 companies in the list. Information was not obtained for five overseas-based companies included in the largest 100 and 17 among the next 150 companies.

Table 9:
Domicile of the Overseas Companies with
UK Investments Included in the Analysis

Number of Companies

USA	39	Denmark	1
Germany	6	Belgium	1
France	3	Sweden	3
Canada	5	Netherlands*	6
Japan	4	Australia	1
Italy	2	Ireland	1
Switzerland	3		
			75

*Including Anglo-Dutch companies.

The sample of UK companies for which accounts were analysed for the estimates reported in Section 4 included most of the UK-based companies with large overseas operations. This does not apply to inward investment; to be included the UK operations had to provide the DAE with copies of their accounts or the accounts for the UK operations for 1989 had to be analysed by the Extel Card Service. Many large overseas companies with operations in the UK do not publish accounts for their UK operations, or the latest accounts available for analysis by Extel were for 1987 or 1988. For a small number of the companies included in the sample, the accounts available for their UK operations did not include all of those operations. (The exact number of companies to which this applies is not known because companies do not state in the accounts of UK subsidiaries whether all the operations of the parent company located in the UK are dealt with in these accounts.) It is not obvious why absence of information for many companies should bias the results, but it could do so; for example, firms making large profits in the UK in relation to the capital they employ here may be shy about publishing their UK results.[1]

[1] A feature of the sample of *UK operations* of overseas companies was the high level of sales per employee. The median level of sales per employee for 72 of the companies for which information on sales per employee was available for their latest accounting year was £114,000, compared with the median for the UK

[*Contd. on p. 54*]

The Data

The principal qualification to the estimates of the value of inward investment included in this section is that the conventions used to estimate profits for the UK operations of companies may be different from those used to assess profits of the parent company. Leaving aside the differing treatment of stocks which are valued on a first-in-first-out (FIFO) basis in the UK and on a last-in-first-out (LIFO) basis in the USA, accounting conventions used in the UK and the USA are broadly similar, but Japanese companies and companies based in Continental Europe prepare their published accounts under significantly different accounting conventions which may, in effect, result in lower estimates of profits. If that is the case, and the profits of UK subsidiaries are calculated according to UK accounting conventions (a realistic assumption), the estimates of the share of UK profits will be exaggerated and too high a proportion of market values will be apportioned to UK operations.

A second qualification to the estimates is that many companies have some flexibility for moving profits from one country to another by their transfer pricing policy for components and products and by making charges for R & D and services provided by the corporate headquarters. One purpose of shifting profits is to minimise tax liabilities. (There is proportionately more scope for moving profits of operations which are small relative to the total operations of the parent. Most of the UK operations of overseas companies are relatively small, compared with the total overseas operations of many UK companies.)

Share prices on 17 May 1990 were used to value the overseas companies and the values were converted to sterling using exchange rates quoted in the *Financial Times* on the same day. The latest published accounts and the accounting period

---

operations of 38 of the UK-based companies whose accounts were analysed in the previous section of £65,000, and the median for the worldwide operations of those companies of £70,000. (The other 102 companies whose accounts were analysed in the previous section did not publish the sales figures of their UK operations and/ or the number of people they employed in the UK.) The difference in UK sales per employee is wide and is unlikely to be wholly explained either by differences in the industrial composition of the two groups of companies or by the employment of sub-contractors. Apart from any differences in efficiency, many of the UK operations of overseas companies distribute goods produced by the parent company elsewhere, as well as manufacturing products in the UK—for example, German chemical companies distribute chemicals manufactured in Germany and American computer companies distribute computer hardware and software made in the USA and other countries through their UK subsidiaries—and turnover per employee would be high for such distribution activities.

nearest to the year ending 31 December 1989 were used for the exercise.

Profits

For 62 of the 75 companies it was possible to use profits earned in the UK and the parent company's profits earned worldwide as the basis for apportionment. Average exchange rates for accounting years were used to convert profits of the overseas companies to sterling in order to compare their profits with the profits of their UK subsidiaries. For 11 companies, sales of the UK operations and worldwide sales were used; for Shell the value of net assets employed and for Unilever an estimate of UK sales were used to apportion market values. The average percentage of UK profits or sales to worldwide profits or sales was 10 per cent, and for only 18 of the 73 companies (excluding the Anglo-Dutch companies) was the percentage above 10 per cent. (For nine companies, either the UK operations or the parent company made losses; where the UK company made losses and the parent did not, either the share in profits of the UK company was taken as zero or sales were used to apportion market value.) Plainly where the proportion of profits attributable to the UK operations is less than, say, 50 per cent (which applies to all but two of the companies), these profits are not the principal determinant of the share prices of the parent company—and this must qualify the result. Although the ratio of stock market prices to earnings is lower for UK than for American companies and companies in some European countries, which suggests that profits earned in the UK are valued less highly, it is not unreasonable to apportion market values on the basis of profits.

Book Value of Parents' Stakes in UK Subsidiary Companies

From the accounts of the UK subsidiary companies it was possible to obtain book values for the stakes of parent companies. (A definition of the book value of stakes is given in Box 2 on page 46.)

Results

The main estimates for inward investment are shown in Table 10. Using profits (or sales) for the UK subsidiaries as a percentage of the worldwide profits (or sales) of the parent companies to apportion stock market values and book values of parent companies' equity, the estimated market value of the 75 UK subsidiaries was £31·3 billion and the *estimated* book value of the equity stakes in the UK subsidiaries was £18·0 billion, giving a

Table 10:
Value of Inward Investment (excluding Banks and Insurance Companies), at 17.5.1990

Countries and Industrial Sectors	Number of Companies	Estimated Market Value	Estimated Book Value	Estimated Market Value as ratio of Estimated Book Value	Actual Book Value Capital and Reserves	Inter-co. Balances
		£ billion			£ billion	
Total	75	31·3	18·0	1·7	13·5	8·9
US companies	39	19·6	10·9	1·8	8·1	3·8
German companies	6	0·7	0·4	1·8	0·5	0·3
Other companies	30	11·0	6·7	1·6	4·9	4·9
Metals	4	0·4	0·3	1·3	0·6	0·0
Chemicals	10	1·9	1·1	1·6	1·1	0·3
Pharmaceuticals	1	0·3	0·2	1·6	0·0	0·1
Engineering including electronics[a]	13	1·4	0·9	1·6	1·2	0·1
Vehicles	8	3·7	3·5	1·0	1·7	2·5
Computers and semi-conductors	9	6·0	3·7	1·6	1·2	0·5
Food, drink and tobacco	6	4·6	1·6	3·0	0·2	2·2
Oil	8	5·5	4·5	1·2	3·7	1·0
Services	6	1·1	0·3	3·7	0·3	-0·1
Other sectors	10	6·4	1·9	3·4	3·5	2·3

[a] Excludes computers and semi-conductors which are shown separately.

valuation ratio of 1·74—a somewhat lower ratio than for UK overseas investment estimated and reported in Section 4.[1] The book value of overseas parent companies' stakes in the capital and reserves of the UK subsidiaries was £13·5 billion compared to the *estimated* book value of the equity stakes for these companies of £18·0 billion. The inter-company balances, the net current and long-term liabilities owed to parent companies, were £8·9 billion; so the *estimated* book value of stakes, £18 billion, lies midway between the actual equity stakes of £13·5 billion and the equity stakes plus the outstanding balances of £8·9 billion = £22·4 billion.[2] When the book value of the equity and reserves (*excluding* the parents' shares of net current and long-term liabilities) reported in the UK subsidiaries' accounts was substituted for the *estimated* book value (estimated by apportioning the book value of the equity of the parent companies), the valuation ratio was higher, 2·3 (31·3:13·5). When the market value of the UK subsidiaries was compared to the book value of the parents's stake in the equity *and* net current and long-term liabilities owed by the UK subsidiaries, the valuation ratio fell to 1·8 ((31·3 + 8·9) : (13·5 + 8·9)). (Net current and long-term liabilities are relatively high for the sample of companies and push down this valuation ratio.)

The valuation ratio is higher for the US-based companies than for the other companies taken together (see Table 10). Estimates of profits for US companies are more reliable because US and UK accounting conventions are similar.

Share prices and exchange rates on 17 May 1990 were used to estimate the value of inward investment. Between 31 December 1989 and 17 May 1990 US share prices—converted to sterling—fell by 4·5 per cent and international share prices converted to sterling and weighted by the country weights shown in Table 12 fell by 6·2 per cent, less than the fall in UK share prices reported on page 45.[3] Between 31 December 1989 and 17 May 1990, sterling rose by 4·1 per cent relative to the US dollar

---

[1] Exchange rates quoted in the *Financial Times* on 17 May 1990 were used to convert share prices and the book value of equity to sterling.

[2] The £8·9 billion seems relatively high, being 66 per cent of the parent companies' stakes in the share capital and reserves of the UK subsidiaries. This compares with 18 per cent for the stock of inward investment at the end of 1987 recorded in *Business Monitor*, MO4, 1987. One partial explanation for the difference is that the ratio increased between the end of 1987 and the end of 1989, the date to which the sample figure relates. The Ford Motor Co., News International and Nestlé accounted for 64 per cent of the £8·9 billion.

[3] The source for international share prices was the FT-Actuaries World Indices published in the *Financial Times*.

Table 11:
Companies with the Largest Inward Investments

	UK Profits as Share of Company's Profits	Estimated Market Value	Estimated Book Value	Investment in UK: Estimated Market Value as ratio of Estimated Book Value	Actual Book Value: Capital and Reserves	Inter-co. Balances
	%	£m.	£m.		£m.	£m.
1. IBM	11·1	4,393	2,542	1·7	882	249
2. Exxon Corp	10·5	3,864	1,890	2·0	1,607	374
3. Nestle	11·2	1,884	664	2·8	−779	2,016
4. Ford UK	13·6	1,836	1,836	1·0	939	2,143
5. Royal Dutch	n.a.	1,811	1,438	1·3	1,447	598
6. American Brands	32·5	1,278	574	2·2	529	100
7. Elf Aquitaine	12·9	1,062	940	1·1	812	8
8. Unilever	n.a.	1,062	255	4·2	n.a.	n.a.
9. Seagram	17·6	842	561	1·5	305	103
10. Eastman Kodak	9·5	741	376	2·0	430	−17

and by 7·6 per cent when weighted by the country weights shown in Table 12.[1]

Table 10 also shows an industrial analysis, but the data should be treated cautiously because of the limited coverage of the sample. Subject to this qualification the importance of inward investment in the computer and semi-conductor and vehicles industries contrasts with their relative insignificance for outward investment. The significance of this contrast is outlined below (page 60). Table 11 lists the companies with the largest inward investments.

There are considerable divergences between the estimated and actual book values of stakes, shown in columns 3, 5 and 6 of Tables 10 and 11. It is not possible to estimate the divergences for outward investment (the subject of Section 4), but they may be less because outward direct investment forms a larger proportion of the assets of UK companies than the UK investments of companies based overseas, which are considered in this section.

Coverage of Inward Investment

At the end of 1989 the book value of inward direct investment by industrial and commercial companies was estimated to be £68·9 billion (Pink Book 1991, p. 60). This estimate excludes investment in banks, other financial institutions and other (property). The CSO has estimated that the 100 overseas-based companies with the largest investments in the UK account for 52 per cent of the total. (Banks were excluded for the purpose of making this estimate but insurance companies were included.) The *estimated* book value of inward investment for the 75 companies, £18·0 billion, was 26 per cent of the official estimate and the actual book value including inter-company balances was about one-third of the official estimate.

The reasons for the shortfall are:

o The omission from the sample of quoted companies for which accounts were not obtained.

o The treatment of the Anglo-Dutch companies (see pages 47 and 48) which has a proportionately larger impact on inward investment.

o The exclusion of unquoted companies, of which the Mars group is a leading example.

---

[1] Use of end-1989 exchange rates to convert apportioned book values, instead of exchange rates on 17 May 1990, would increase the estimated total book value of inward investment by about 5 per cent, from £18 billion to about £19 billion.

Investments in North Sea Oil and Gas

At book values inward investment in the oil industry *including* North Sea oil accounted for about a quarter of total inward investment at the end of 1989. As a check on this important element of inward investment, the market to book value ratios for some UK companies which specialise in North Sea exploration and development were examined. At 17 May 1990, the ratios for Lasmo, Enterprise and Sovereign were 1·7, 5·1 and 2·2 and averaged 3·0 when weighted by book values of the companies' share capital and reserves, suggesting a multiple of more than two for converting investment in North Sea oil at book value to market value.

The Effects of Direct Investment

During the course of the study a good deal of information about UK overseas and inward investment was perused. Although an overall assessment of the effects of overseas and inward investment would go beyond the assessment of the effects on the balance of payments which are the subject of this paper, it is clear that there are major differences between outward and inward investment. Britain's outward investment is by companies which are internationally competitive in their trades, of which pharmaceutical companies are an outstanding example, followed by the food, drink and tobacco companies. Similarly, much of the inward investment is in trades in which companies based in the UK have been weak— here the motor industry is the leading example. In many industries there is a two-way flow of capital, but the international flows of capital do enable UK companies which have advantages to use those advantages in overseas markets and for companies based overseas with advantages in industries and trades in which UK companies are weaker to invest in the UK.

Summary

The estimates reported in this section again show that market values of direct investment are substantially higher than book values. There are qualifications to these estimates because of the lower coverage of total inward investment and the use of different accounting conventions by companies based in other countries; nevertheless, the estimates indicate that the mark-up of market values over book values is of the same order of magnitude as that for outward investment.

SIX

The American Method of Valuing Direct Investment

Introduction

The Bank of England reported the results of a preliminary exercise to revalue direct investment by disaggregating asset stocks by country and revaluing them through time using appropriate share price indices in its *Quarterly Bulletin* for November 1990. When the Bank made these estimates, the DAE method had not been used to value inward investment and an advantage of the American method which was used by the Bank of England was that it provided estimates of market values for both outward and inward investment. The Bank concluded from its preliminary revaluation exercise that: 'This approach yields the result that the "true" net asset position (for direct investment) may be less advantageous than presently recorded', rather than an under-estimate of the true position. (The percentage mark-up of book values for inward investment was so much greater than for outward investment that the revaluation of inward investment at the end of 1988 exceeded that for outward investment, though the book value of outward investment was much greater than that for inward investment.) The Bank described the method as 'one of the simplest', but acknowledged that its approach involved a 'highly complex' exercise, that it was 'flawed' and that it was not a definitive exercise.

For an 'outsider' there are considerable statistical problems in replicating the exercise performed by the Bank; these problems are listed in Appendix B describing the data requirements and problems entailed in using the method; however, it is understood that the Bank used only data which had been published. In a rough and ready way the Bank's exercise was duplicated.

Share Price Movements

The underlying explanation for the results obtained by the Bank is that UK share prices which are used to provide a hypothetical indicator of the market value of *inward* investment, have risen more rapidly than share prices in countries which are hosts for UK direct

Ploughed-back Profits and Share Price Indices

Retained profits are additions to investment and are treated as a component of direct investment flows for the official statistics. In order to avoid double-counting it is necessary to exclude retained profits from new investment flows or from capital gains, preferably the former. For estimating market values of US direct investment, Professor Eisner has used Morgan Stanley indices of stock market prices adjusted for ploughed-back profits. Professor Eisner provided the author with these data. To calculate share price indices, the percentage of retained profits was deducted from the index:

Where retained profits as a percentage of share prices are re and P is the unadjusted share price index, then P_a the adjusted index is:

$$Pa_t = (1 - \frac{re_t}{100}) \ Pa_{t-1} \times \frac{P}{P_{t-1}}$$

For the initial period $P_a = P$.

Changes in share prices adjusted for retained profits reflect revaluations of assets not included in ploughed-back profits and changes in the value of intangible assets which in turn reflect the expected future profits of a company.

investment overseas. The comparisons are shown in Tables 12 and 13 (pp. 64, 65); the first Table shows share price indices in terms of domestic currencies, and the second gives the indices in sterling after adjustment for changes in exchange rates, the relevant comparison for the exercise. The countries included are the principal host countries for UK direct investment overseas and account for about two-thirds of it. (The source of inward investment does not affect the results of this exercise.) The indices of share prices used for the estimates given in the first three rows of Tables 12 and 13 are the statistics of industrial share prices published by the IMF. Row 4 of both tables is based on the indices prepared by Morgan Stanley which were used by Eisner and Pieper (1991).

Morgan Stanley also estimate ploughed-back profits as a percentage of share prices; this information was used to calculate the adjusted share price indices shown in row 5 of each table, and these exclude ploughed-back profits. The derivation of the index is described in Box 3 (opposite page). The final three rows of the tables show indices for the period December 1974 or the end of 1974 to December 1988 or end of 1988 because the Bank of England used the period end-1974 to end-1988 for its exercise.

The comparisons given in Table 12 show that the UK share price index has increased faster than share price indices for stock markets of the other countries included in the Table. (The final column gives a weighted average for the other countries.) The comparisons in Table 13 show that prices on overseas share markets when converted to sterling rose more slowly than UK share prices over the period 1964 to 1989, but that between 1980 and 1989, the weighted average increase for overseas markets was *above* that for the UK. Another feature of the Table is that the result of adjusting the indices to exclude ploughed-back profits is to boost the indices for the other countries relative to that for the UK—the weighted average for the other countries for the period end-1974 to end-1988 is raised from 42 to 50 per cent of that for the UK (see the last two rows of the final column of Table 13). One reason why the adjustments may reduce share price indices for the UK more than for the other countries is that UK inflation was faster, and so inflationary stock 'profits' were greater and were ploughed back. Also, US accounting procedures, and in particular the LIFO treatment of stocks, exclude most stock profits.

Another important determinant of the revaluations using share price indices is the timing of investment flows—in broad terms, the longer investments have been in place the greater will be the appreciation. Table 14 (page 66) reports the flows of direct investment since the end of 1964. (For this Table flows of investment *include* changes in amounts owed to parent companies as well as changes in share capital and reserves.) The pattern of aggregate outward and inward investment is very similar and so it should not greatly affect the results of the exercise.

A third determinant of the extent of revaluations is the split between investment in the share capital and reserves of subsidiaries and the amounts owed to parent companies which are included as investments in overseas foreign subsidiaries or associate companies; for the exercise reported below the amounts owed to parent companies were assumed to be fixed in money terms and not to move with share price indices. Table 15 (page 67)

63

Table 12:
Movements of Share Prices, 1964 to 1989

Period	UK	USA	Netherlands	Australia	Canada	Germany	France	Weighted Average (as percentage of UK)
Weights[1]		42	26	12	9	6	5	100
				Percentage Change				
1. 1964-89	976	329	235	538	352	172	587	235 (34)
2. 1980-89	297	175	286	153	83	166	328	200 (67)
3. Dec. 1974-Dec. 1988	1386	327	264	624	300	172	601	348 (25)
4. End 1974 to end 1988 – Morgan Stanley indices unadjusted	1170	263	412	629	283	207	611	361 (31)
5. End 1974 to end 1988 – Morgan Stanley indices adjusted[2]	371	63	157	245	79	54	341	124 (33)

[1] Weights are based on overseas investment at the end of 1987 and exclude amounts due to parent on inter-company account. (*Source: Business Monitor MO4*, 1987, Table 9, pp. 29, 30.)

[2] Adjusted to exclude ploughed-back profits from the indices.

Sources: For share prices, rows 1-3: 'Index numbers of industrial share prices', as given in the *Int. Fin. Stats. Yearbook* for 1989 and issues of *Int. Fin. Stats.* (The index numbers are averages for years or for the month of December.)

Table 13:
Movements of Share Prices, 1964 to 1989 (in Sterling)

	UK	USA	Netherlands	Australia	Canada	Germany	France	Weighted Average (as percentage of UK)
Weights		42	26	12	9	6	5	100
Period				*Percentage Change*				
1. 1964-89	976	631	872	1134	602	880	800	775 (79)
2. 1980-89	297	291	413	298	157	265	303	311 (105)
3. Dec. 1974-Dec. 1988	1386	444	496	502	321	384	574	456 (33)
4. End 1974 to end 1988 – Morgan Stanley indices unadjusted	1170	371	733	510	313	439	576	490 (42)
5. End 1974 to end 1988 – Morgan Stanley indices adjusted	371	112	318	189	93	171	319	187 (50)

Table 14:
Flows of Direct Investment,[a] **1965-69 to 1985-89**

| | Outward | | Inward | |
	£bn.	Percentage of total	£bn.	Percentage of total
1965-69	3·6	2·5	2·4	3·1
1970-74	10·2	7·1	5·8	7·6
1975-79	20·7	14·5	10·4	13·5
1980-84	26·4	18·5	13·5	17·6
1985-89	82·1	57·4	44·7	58·7
	143·0	100	76·8	100

[a] There is a break in the series in 1979; the earlier figures were doubled to make them approximately consistent with later figures which are more comprehensive in terms of industries included.

Sources: Pink Books for 1963-73, 1980 and 1991.

shows the breakdown for the financing of outward and inward direct investment in 1987; a higher percentage of outward investment is indebtedness and this damps down the revaluation effect for outward investment.

The Results

Table 16 (page 68) summarises the results of the exercise using the Morgan Stanley indices to replicate the procedure used by the Bank of England, but based on a different period—from the end of 1964 to the end of 1989. The first six rows of the Table show revaluations for investments in the six countries where the largest UK direct investments overseas are located. In brief, the unadjusted hypothetical market values shown in column 2 are calculated by assuming the flows of investment excluding increases in amounts owed to parent companies and after deducting revaluations which include write-offs are invested and appreciate in line with the unadjusted Morgan Stanley indices. The hypothetical, market value of outward investment located in the countries listed was £187·7 billion (Table 16, row 7, column 2) compared with a book value of £89·5 billion (row 7, column 1), giving a ratio of 2·1 (row 7, column 5). For inward investment the ratio was 2·97 (row 10, column 5). The use of stock market indices to revalue direct investment boosts values of inward investment more than values of outward invest-

Table 15:
The Financing of Direct Investment in 1987

	Outward Investment	Inward Investment
	£bn. (percentages of total)	
Share capital and reserves	51·1 (74)	36·3 (85)
Net current and long-term liabilities owed to parent companies	17·5 (26)	6·6 (15)
Total	68·6 (100)	42·9 (100)

Source: Business Monitor MO4, 1987.

ment; the lower mark-up for overseas investment than inward investment reflects the low mark-up for the large UK direct investments in the USA, the high proportion of overseas investment accounted for by debt which is assumed not to appreciate with share indices, and the write-offs of overseas investments.

For row 8 of Table 16, it is *assumed* that the percentage revaluations if share price indices were used for the countries not included earlier in the Table are the same as those calculated for the countries included in rows 1 to 6 of the Table, *apart* from the USA. The effect of this procedure is to raise the ratio of the market value to book value for overseas investment to 2·28 (row 9, column 5 of Table 16). The data shown in Table C.2 and commented upon in Appendix C lend some support to this procedure.[1] On average the investment in the other countries is older—a factor which boosts the revaluation effect.

The result of the exercise is that the balance of outward over inward investment, net direct investment, is reduced from £39·6 billion to £29·3 billion. Whether the result of such an exercise is to make the balance of the hypothetical, market value of outward over the value of inward investment 'less advantageous' (to use the Bank of England's term) than the balance of book values, depends, in part, on the initial and terminal date for the exercise which determines the levels of share prices and exchange rates used. The exercise reported upon in Table 16, was started from 1964 because there is detailed information about direct investment for

---

[1] The other countries include tax havens such as Bermuda which account for about 4 per cent of UK overseas investment and for which there are no stock market indices.

Table 16:
Exercise to Value Direct Investment Using Share Price Indices from the end of 1964 to the end of 1989*

	(1) Book value end-1989[a] £bn.	(2) Unadjusted hypothetical market value[b] £bn.	(3) Adjusted hypothetical market value[c] £bn.	(4) (3) with revaluations from 1985 to 1989 added	(5) (2) as a ratio of (1)	(6) (3) as a ratio of (1)	(7) (4) as a ratio of (1)
Outward investment							
1. USA	53·0	88·7	69·0		1·67	1·30	
2. Australia	10·2	30·9	16·7		3·03	1·64	
3. Netherlands	9·0	18·8	14·1		2·09	1·57	
4. Canada	6·7	17·7	9·8		2·64	1·46	
5. France	6·3	18·6	13·3		2·95	2·11	
6. Germany	*4·3*	*13·0*	*7·3*		*3·02*	*1·70*	
7. Total for countries listed only	89·5	187·7	130·2		2·10	1·45	
8. Other countries[d]	*37·1*	*100·6*	*62·2*		*2·71*	*1·68*	
9. Total outward investment	126·6	288·3	192·4	220·0	2·28	1·52	1·74
10. *Inward investment*	*87·0*	*259·0*	*150·0*	*141·8*	*2·97*	*1·72*	*1·63*
11. *Net investment*	*39·6*	*29·3*	*42·4*	*78·2*	*0·74*	*1·07*	*1·97*

[a] Total direct investment less other (property) which was estimated for investment overseas.

[b] The hypothetical market values are based on end-1989 stock market prices.

[c] Adjusted market values exclude ploughed-back profits from indices.

[d] Market values for other countries are assumed to move with the weighted average for the countries listed, excluding the USA.

* *Note:* There are serious qualifications to the data used to make the estimates reported in this Table. The qualifications are described in the text, page 71, and in Appendix B.

Source: Pink Book 1991, Table 8.2A, and *Overseas Direct Investment* (1989).

that year in the Reddaway (1968) and Steuer (1973) reports. The Bank used the period end-1974 to end-1988 and, as shown in Tables 12 and 13, this does boost the relative revaluation of inward investment—the explanation for this result is that UK share prices were far below trend in December 1974. The Bank started their exercise from the end of 1974 because that was the first year for which reliable official data on stocks and flows of investment were available. Similarly, the final date influences the result as shown below.

Qualifications to the Estimates

The exercise suggested a number of qualifications to estimates of market values constructed using the American method.

1. For both the Bank's preliminary exercise and the exercise reported in column 2 of Table 16, ploughed-back profits are treated as new investment and are assumed to rise in line with share prices. However, one reason for the rise in share prices is retained profits, so there is an element of double-counting, and this is important because in a majority of years ploughed-back profits represented more than half of outward investment. The double-counting also explains why the multiples of market values to book values given by the American method are higher than the multiples obtained by the DAE method. When the exercise was re-run for *inward* investment using the *adjusted* Morgan Stanley index for the UK, which excludes ploughed-back profits, the multiple was reduced from 2·97 to 1·72 (row 10, columns 5 and 6 of Table 16). When similar indices were used for the other countries, the multiple for outward investment fell from 2·28 to 1·52 (row 9) and for net investment increased from 0·74 to 1·07—that is, the value of net investment was above the book value: £42·4 billion compared to £39·6 billion.[1]

2. There are more (and proportionately more) revaluations involving write-offs of goodwill arising on, or after, acquisition for UK overseas investment than for inward investment. These

---

[1] Eisner and Pieper (1991) used the same stock market indices, and their estimate of the market value (using an adjusted index of UK share prices) of US investment in the UK was £97 billion at the end of 1989 compared to a book value of £61 billion, giving a ratio of 1·6—this compares with the ratio for *total* inward investment to the UK of 1·63 (Table 16, row 10, final column). US investment accounts for about 40 per cent of the total and it is probably older than the average for total inward investment, a factor which would increase the ratio for US investment in the UK.

write-offs are treated as negative investment for the exercise because published data for aggregate stocks of overseas investment at book values are calculated net of these revaluations (write-offs); they reduce the share capital and reserves (including retained profits) component of overseas investment, and *dampen* the revaluation of overseas investment.[1] The revaluations, which include changes in values caused by changes in exchange rates and other causes besides write-offs, are substantial. Separate estimates of write-offs alone are not available. Adding back the official estimates of revaluations for 1985 to 1989, which exaggerates the adjustment because revaluations caused by exchange rate changes are included as well as write-offs, raises the ratio for outward investment from 1·52 (row 9, column 6 of Table 16) to 1·74 (row 9, column 7) above that for inward investment, 1·63 (row 10, column 7), and raises the ratio for net investment to 1·97 (row 11, column 7).[2] The earlier results showing a greater increase in hypothetical market value for inward investment than for outward investment is reversed.

3. There are two components of a company's stake in its subsidiaries measured at book value—its interest in the share capital and reserves and the net amounts due to the parent company from the subsidiaries. (As was shown earlier in Table 15, the proportion of direct investment overseas which was financed by amounts 'owed to parent companies' was higher than the proportion for direct inward investment.) It was assumed for the exercise reported on in Table 16 that amounts due to parent companies do not move with the market; they are fixed in money terms, but the Bank included them as equity investments subject to appreciation in line with share price indices for its exercise. It is necessary to consider why the proportion is higher for overseas investment. If UK firms were exporting more goods and services through their overseas

---

[1] It is understood that the Bank ignored such revaluations and write-offs for their exercise; they did not treat them as negative investment and this is the correct procedure unless the write-offs are of an exceptional nature and reflect real events of a sort which would not have an impact on the general run of companies to which share price indices relate but do reduce the value of overseas investments.

[2] If the purpose of the exercise was to assess market values relative to cost—the extent of appreciation of investments— the write-offs would be added to the book values of the investments, but the purpose here is to compare market values to the actual book values of investments as recorded in official statistics, and so the write-offs are not added back to the book values of the investments.

subsidiaries, relative to the capital of the subsidiaries, and compared to imports through the UK subsidiaries of overseas-based companies, that could explain the existence of higher amounts owed to the UK parent companies. In practice, this seems an unlikely explanation because sales per employee are higher for inward investments, probably, in part, because of a high level of imports from group companies.[1]

As noted in Box 2 (pp. 46-47), whether, and to what extent, subsidiaries are financed by share capital, retained profits or 'accounts due to parents' is, in part, a matter of choice rather than principle. UK companies could rely more heavily on balances due to parents, so the exclusion of these balances from equity investment could lead to a relative underestimate of values for overseas investment compared to inward investment. Put another way, where a company finances its subsidiaries by increasing loans to it, or increasing the accounts due from it, its investment in the share capital and reserves of subsidiaries is more highly geared and could be expected to increase in value in percentage terms, more rapidly than if the company had financed its subsidiaries with a higher proportion of share capital and reserves.

4. The high level of overseas and inward investment for the Netherlands reflects the treatment of the Anglo-Dutch companies Royal Dutch-Shell and Unilever. If these investments were treated on a net basis, both inward and outward investment would be reduced and the effect of revaluations to increase the value of inward investment relative to outward may be smaller because share price indices for the Netherlands rose more slowly than indices for the UK.

5. To perform the exercise it was necessary to make many assumptions, even guesses, about the multiple of stock market prices to book values at the end of 1964 and the flow of investments in order to balance flows of investment with stock figures available for benchmark years (see Appendix B for a description of the data problems). Finally, some stock figures had to be divided between investment in shares and reserves and net accounts due to parents. Although these assumptions

---

[1] The division between share capital and net current and long-term liabilities owed to group companies varies; for direct investments (excluding investments in financial services) in the USA, net current and long-term liabilities represented 80 per cent of share capital at the end of 1987, compared to 10·4 per cent for Canadian investments and an overall average of 34 per cent.

made the calculations unreliable, they probably do not affect the broad results of the exercise.

6. New investments made in the form of take-overs usually involve paying a premium over market values (see page 27). If these investments could be isolated, they could be discounted before applying market indices to them. However, if such adjustments were made they would apply to both inward and outward investments and again would probably not affect the broad results of the exercise.

7. In some years more than half of inward direct investment was in the oil industry and this is only one example, though the most important one, of the uneven distribution of direct investments. National indices of industrial share prices do not provide a fair guide to the market value of such investments.

Summary

In brief, the results the Bank obtained from its preliminary exercise were flawed for the reasons it gave. The exercise has been developed in the ways described in this section.

(a) The Bank used a period which was particularly favourable for UK share prices. (In this section the effects of using other periods has been shown.)

(b) There was an element of double-counting of ploughed-back profits in the Bank's exercise which boosted the final multiples applied to book values for both inward and outward investment. (This qualification was avoided in this section by using indices of share prices which exclude ploughed-back profits.)

Problems remain, however:

o The duplication of holdings of the Anglo-Dutch companies probably boosts the revaluation of inward relative to outward investment.

o The use of broad share indices is unsatisfactory because inward investment and UK investment overseas are concentrated in certain industries. (This qualification is more important for the UK than for the USA with its wider spread of direct investment.)

o The treatment of *increases* in the amounts due to parent companies all of which were excluded from flows of capital which appreciate in line with stock market prices for the exercise reported in this section resulted in an under-estimation of the market value of investments.

o The data used for the exercise are subject to numerous qualifications which are listed in Appendix B and which reduce the credibility of the results.

The comparisons of changes in share prices shown in Table 13 suggest that the difference in appreciation between UK shares and the weighted averages for overseas share markets was not large over the 1980s or from 1964 to 1989. Exclusion of ploughed-back profits from share price indices reduces the increases shown by the indices and the differences between the increases for UK share prices and those for other countries taken together, so the multiples of market to book value for overseas and inward investment are not very different. The calculations using adjusted share price indices reported in Table 16 suggest a multiple of stock-market to book values of less than two at the end of 1989 while the estimates with revaluations—write-offs—added back suggest that the effects of revaluation are similar for outward and inward investment.

There are many qualifications to the exercises reported in this section, but for what they are worth, they suggest a lower multiple of market to book value for direct investment overseas than the estimate made using the DAE method, which was also qualified. The main explanation is that different share prices are used to measure the market value of overseas investments: UK share prices for the DAE method and share prices for the overseas host countries for the American method. For the reasons given on pages 40 and 41, the use of UK share prices (the DAE method) is the more satisfactory approach. Other possible explanations for the difference are that share prices of companies with overseas investments outperformed others, or that successful UK companies whose share prices increased faster than average, increased their overseas operations. If these explanations are correct, then the DAE-type estimates provide more accurate measures of market values.[1]

---

[1] A careful reader may suspect that there is an inconsistency between the results of adjusting direct investment by share price indices in this section and the large capital gains on portfolio investment in equities reported in Table 2. One explanation for the difference is that the ratio of inward to outward direct investment at 0·7 at the end of 1979 was much higher than the ratio of inward to outward portfolio investment in equities (0·39) and the ratio for inward to outward portfolio investment in equities between the end of 1979 and the end of 1984 (0·2).

SEVEN

Estimates of the Value of Direct Investment

The DAE Method

In this section the estimates reported in Sections 4 and 5 are used to estimate the market value of the UK's net direct investment. A check on these estimates is then made using the CSO's estimates of the income obtained from direct investment. The principal bugbear for estimating the market value of direct investments from official statistics by the DAE method is to tie the estimates of market values and book values of overseas investments which were given in Sections 4 and 5 into the book values of overseas investment given in 'The Pink Book 1991: United Kingdom Balance of Payments'. Direct estimates of the book values of UK companies' stakes in the capital, loans, and outstanding accounts of their overseas subsidiaries are not available from the published accounts of most of the UK parent companies, but they are available for inward direct investment and were reported in Section 5. The estimates for inward investment indicate that when stakes are measured by parents' stakes in the equity of subsidiaries, this gives a lower estimate of the book value of stakes than that given by the DAE method of apportioning the total book value of parents' equity, while the inclusion of net debt in the stakes gives a higher figure. The boost given to estimates of overseas investment stakes by the inclusion of net debt reduces the multiple of book values of stakes used to revalue stakes at market values.

The sector analysis of direct investment for 1989 given in the Pink Book is reproduced as column 1 of Table 17 (with estimated outward investment in property, £3·2 billion, and inward investment in 'other property', £6·3 billion, excluded). Column 2 shows a first crude estimate of market values. The DAE method suggests that the market value of overseas investment is about twice the book value and this multiple is used for both outward and inward investment, although the calculations given in Section 5 suggest the multiple could be lower for inward investment, and it is further

Table 17:
Direct Investment – Sector Analysis, 1989

	(1) At book value	(2) Estimated market value £ billion	(3) Difference (2)–(1)
Investment overseas			
By:			
UK banks	4·9	4·9	0
Other financial institutions	12·3 }		
Industrial and commercial companies	109·0 }	242·6	121·3
Total UK assets	126·2	247·5	121·3
*Investment in UK by overseas residents**			
In:			
UK Banks	8·4	8·4	0
Other financial institutions	9·7 }		
Industrial and commercial companies	68·9 }	157·2	78·2
Total	87·0	165·6	78·6
Balance	39·3	81·9	42·6
Balance after deducting 'other property'	36·2		

*'other property' is excluded.

Source: For column 1: Pink Book, Table 8.2A, total UK direct investment less other (property) which was estimated for investment overseas.

assumed that investment by UK banks and in UK banks is worth book values.[1]

The effect of the revaluations is to increase UK net direct investment overseas by £42·6 billion. A qualification to these estimates is that the market valuation multiple is applied to the stakes of the UK parents including the net loans and outstanding

---

[1] Valuation ratios—stock market value as a ratio of book value—for UK banks averaged approximately 1 in May 1990 and it is thought that overseas investments in UK banking were not worth more than book values in May 1990. Many overseas banks have made losses on their UK operations.

accounts owed by the subsidiaries to parents. In Table 18 an estimate of these loans and accounts is made for 1989 using data for 1987 published in *Business Monitor*, MO4, 1987—the split shown for 1987 in MO4 1987 is applied to the 1989 estimates of investment given in The Pink Book 1991. The effect of replacing book values by estimated market values is reduced from £42·6 billion in Table 17 to £25·5 billion in Table 18. The revaluation to convert book values to market values is lower because only the share capital and reserves element of investment is boosted—amounts owed to parents are excluded from the revaluation, and because a higher proportion of outward investment at book value is amounts owed to parents than for inward investment. The significance of the combination of equity and amounts owed to parents has been discussed earlier in the paper (Section 6, pages 70 and 71). The best estimate of the revaluation based on the DAE method would lie between £25·5 billion and £42·6 billion—perhaps the average, £34 billion.

One argument for taking a figure between the two estimates is that a part of the outstanding accounts owed to parent companies is capital rather than outstanding trade debtors and in principle should be included in the estimates of the book value of capital made by the DAE method. The ratios of total assets to stakes for outward investment described in Appendix A on page 106 point to a similar conclusion. It could be argued that the £34 billion is a cautious estimate because the same multiple of two has been used to convert investment in the share capital and reserves of subsidiaries at book values to market values in the exercise shown in Table 17; the estimates reported in Sections 4 and 5 suggest a lower multiple would be appropriate for inward investment, and this would reduce the revaluation of inward relative to overseas investment. Also, large write-downs have been applied to outward investment and positive revaluations to inward investment.

The American method based on the use of Morgan Stanley indices gave a lower multiple for direct investment overseas—the adjusted market value was 1·52 times the book value (Table 16, row 9 column 6) and 1·72 for inward investment, but this difference was reversed when write-offs were added back. There are many qualifications to both sets of estimates, but possible explanations for the estimates for direct investment overseas obtained by the DAE method being higher than those based on the use of the American method and reasons for giving preference to the DAE method were given on page 73.

Table 18:
Direct Investment by Industrial and Commercial Companies: Analysis by Type of Stake, 1989

	(1) At book value	(2) Estimated market values £ billion	(3) Difference (2)–(1)
Investment overseas:			
Industrial and commercial companies			
Interest of parent companies in:			
share capital and reserves of subsidiaries	109·0 { 81·1[a]	162·2	81·1
net current and long-term liabilities	27·9[a]	27·9	0
	109·0	190·1	81·1
Other financial institutions	12·3	24·6	12·3
	121·3	214·7	93·4
Investment in the UK by overseas residents:			
Industrial and commercial companies			
Interest of foreign parent companies in:			
share capital and reserves of subsidiaries	68·9 { 58·2[b]	116·4	58·2
net current and long-term liabilities	10·7[b]	10·7	0
	68·9	127·1	58·2
Other financial institutions	9·7	19·4	9·7
	78·6	146·5	67·9
Balance	42·7	68·2	25·5

Note on the share capital rows: the book-value column shows the subsidiary figures 81·1 / 27·9 (overseas) and 58·2 / 10·7 (UK), with overall totals 121·3 and 78·6 respectively.

[a] £109 bn. split in the ratio 51·1 : 17·5 (*Business Monitor MO4*, 1987, p. 35, line 3, col. 4 and 5).

[b] £68·9 bn. split in the ratio 36·3 : 6·6 (*Business Monitor MO4*, 1987, p. 53, line 6, col. 4 and 5).

Table 19:
Earnings on Direct Investment in 1989

78

	(1)	(2)	Book value of overseas investment (3)	Market value of overseas investment if M.V./E ratio is 11:1 (4)	Market value of overseas investment if M.V./E ratio is 11:1 (interest excluded) (5)	Net loans and outstanding accounts (6)	Total (7)
				£ billion			
Earnings on investment overseas:							
Unremitted profits	9·1						
Dividends remitted	5·9						
Net interest received	0·9	16·7	129·4	183·7	173·8	30·9[b]	204·7
Profits of branches	0·8						
Other	0·0						
Earnings of overseas residents on direct investment in the UK:							
In non-oil companies:							
Unremitted profits	1·9						
Dividends remitted	3·3						
Net interest paid	0·7						
Profits of branches	−0·3	8·9	93·3	97·9	90·2	10·7[b]	100·9
In oil companies:							
Unremitted profits	1·7						
Dividends and interest remitted[a]	1·5						
Other	0·1						
Balance			36·1	85·8	83·6	20·2	103·8

Notes: [a] For this exercise the £1·5bn. is assumed to be dividends, i.e. to include no interest.   [b] These estimates are taken from Table 18.

A Check Using Capitalised Earnings

An obvious check on these estimates of the market value is to capitalise the income from direct investment. The calculations are shown in Table 19. A market value to earnings ratio of 11·0 was used which compares with the price to earnings ratio (P/E ratio) of 10·75 for the 500 FT-Actuaries share index on 17 May 1990.[1] It is assumed that the same market value to earnings multiple applies to both outward and inward investment; as, in practice, P/E ratios for US companies are higher than for UK companies, and the ratio of share prices to declared profits per share are higher for companies based in other European countries, there is a case for using a higher market value to earnings ratio for outward investment instead of applying the same multiple.

Column (3) of Table 19 shows the effects of applying the multiple to total earnings on overseas and inward investment shown in column (2); the estimated market value of net investment is £85·8 billion (second figure in final row, 'balance') compared to a book value of £36·1 billion (first figure in final row), giving a ratio of 2·38 for market to book value. For the remaining columns of the Table interest and net loans and outstanding accounts are separated. The final estimate of market value of overseas invest-ment, after adding back net long-term and other balances owed to the parent companies, again shows a very substantial increase in valuation—nearly trebling the value of Britain's net direct investment overseas. However, there are qualifications to the estimates of interest (see footnote (a) to Table 18) and the estimation of net loans, etc. (see footnote (b) to Table 18, footnote (b) to Table 17, and the text, pages 70 and 71).

There are serious qualifications to the estimates and there are differences in coverage between Tables 17 and 18 and Table 19. An obvious explanation for differences in valuation between those shown in Tables 17 and 18 and Table 19 is that the P/E ratio for companies with overseas investments could be higher than the market value to earnings ratio on which the calculations shown in Table 19 are based.[2] A notable feature of the revaluations based upon the capitalisation of earnings is that the value of overseas investments is boosted proportionately more than inward

---

[1] The P/E ratio on 17 May 1990 was used as a basis for the estimates, rather than the 12·5 applying at 31 December 1989, for consistency with the estimates of market values using the DAE method.

[2] The weighted average P/E ratio at 17 May 1990 for the sample of companies whose accounts were analysed in Section 4 was 12·3 compared to the P/E ratio for the 500 share index of 11·5.

Table 20:
Earnings from Overseas and Inward Direct Investment

	Earnings from: Outward Direct Investment[1]	Inward Direct Investment[1]	(of which oil companies)	Market value of net investment if P/E 11:1	Book value of net direct investment[2]
			£ billion		
1979	5·82	4·00	(1·92)	20·0	9·9
1980	5·05	4·77	(2·90)	3·1	8·1
1981	5·42	4·70	(2·73)	7·9	10·9
1982	4·81	4·67	(2·58)	0·4	17·3
1983	6·20	5·27	(2·95)	10·2	20·2
1984	7·80	6·28	(3·31)	16·9	27·8
1985	7·75	7·51	(4·00)	2·6	30·9
1986	7·80	5·19	(2·20)	28·7	29·9
1987	10·94	6·85	(2·65)	45·0	29·3
1988	13·85	8·33	(1·97)	60·7	29·1
1989	16·67	8·88	(3·20)	85·7	34·5

[1] *Source*: Pink Book, Table 5.2.

[2] Average of book values at the beginning and end of each year. (*Source*: Pink Book, Table 8.1).

investment—outward investment is increased by 58 per cent compared with an increase of 8 per cent for inward investment.[1] (The difference reflects the lower earnings in relation to book values in 1989 on inward, compared to outward, investment.)[2]

The net difference between the mark-ups on direct overseas investment and inward direct investment calculated using a constant price/earnings ratio varies sharply through time as earnings, particularly earnings on inward investment in North Sea oil and gas exploration and extraction, change. The estimates are

[1] $\dfrac{\text{Col 7} - \text{Col 3}}{\text{Col 3}} \times 100.$

[2] This result is not peculiar to 1989—for the three years 1987 to 1989, earnings on overseas direct investments averaged 13·0 per cent per year, compared to 10·9 per cent per year for inward investment (*Source for data*: Pink Book 1991). The point is reinforced by the higher price/ earnings (P/E) ratios for shares in the USA and some other overseas share markets, compared to the UK market.

Table 21:
Dividends from Direct Investment in 1989

	Net dividends	Gross equivalent	Capitalised on a yield of 4·83%[1]	Overseas Investment Capitalised on a yield of 2·47%[2]
			£ billion	
Dividends remitted on:				
Overseas investment	5·9	7·9	163·6	319·8
Inward investment	4·8[3]	6·4	132·5	132·5
Balance	1·1	1·5	31·1	187·3

[1] The gross yield for the UK 500 share index.

[2] The gross yield for the FT – Actuaries World Index.

[3] Includes interest remitted by oil companies which is not separated from dividends.

shown in Table 20; between 1980 and 1986 the estimated market value of net investment was *below* the book value. If in the future the price of oil were to, say, quadruple, profits from North Sea investments would increase and so would the market value of the investments, but the higher oil price would result in higher prices for Britain's net energy exports. For Table 20 the multiple for profits from North Sea investments is assumed to be the same as that for other investments but oil reserves are a wasting asset and so profits from extracting oil would be priced on a lower market value to earnings ratio.

Capitalising Dividends

Capitalising dividends suggests itself as an alternative source of estimates of market values. The results of such an exercise are shown in Table 21. Dividends are capitalised, firstly, using the gross dividend yield for the 500 Share Index and, secondly, using the gross dividend yield for the FT-Actuaries World Indices for overseas investment. Again the calculations suggest direct investment is undervalued. When the same dividend yield is used for both outward and inward investment the effect on inward investment is large relative to that on outward investment compared to the earlier exercises because a higher proportion of profits on inward investment is paid out as dividends. An important qualification to these estimates is that UK companies may use different criteria when fixing the dividends their overseas subsidiaries should pay out relative to their profits, than the criteria used by independent overseas companies when deciding upon their dividends.

Conclusion
Estimates of the market value of net UK direct investment based upon capitalising income flows indicate a substantially higher value than estimates using the DAE method.

PART THREE:

Revised Estimates of Britain's Balance of Payments and Conclusions

EIGHT

Revised Estimates of Britain's Balance-of-Payments Record during the 1980s

The Effects of the Revisions

The purpose of this section is to present revisions of the official estimates of Britain's balance-of-payments record during the 1980s using the estimates of the market values of direct investment reported in Section 7. For the revised estimates of capital gains of £82·3 billion shown in Table 22 a multiple of 1·75 is used to convert the total of net direct investment at book values at the end of 1989, £36·2 billion, to market prices, and the same multiple is used for revising *both* the 1979 and 1989 estimates. The estimates reported in Part 2 of this paper show that the valuation of direct investment at book values is below market values, but it has not been possible to estimate a precise multiple to convert book values at the end of 1989 to market values. The estimates based on the DAE method suggest a revaluation of the order of £34 billion for converting book values of direct investment to market values (see page 76), but a revision of +£27·2 billion has been used here to avoid any impression that the revised estimates suffer from 'over-egging'.[1] The estimates of capital values based upon capitalising income suggest that the £27·2 billion estimate is very cautious.

The effects of the revisions are to raise the value of net direct investment at the end of 1989 by £27·2 billion, nominal capital gains to £82·3 billion during the 1980s and Britain's net external assets at the end of 1989 to £110·9 billion. If all of the balancing item for the 1980s, £26·0 billion, is assumed to be unrecorded borrowing (see page 28), net assets at the end of 1989 were £84·9 billion (£110·9 billion − £26 billion).[2]

---

[1] The multiple for 1979 may be lower than the assumed 1·75 because share prices rose steeply during the 1980s, raising the multiple, and the oil price was high at the end of 1979, lifting the value of inward investment in North Sea oil exploration and development.

[2] No allowance has been made for defaults—capital losses—on third world debts of UK banks. If the provisions made by UK banks were treated as capital losses, these would reduce the capital gains during the 1980s and the UK's net assets at the end of 1989.

Table 22:
Revised Estimates of Britain's Balance of Payments Record during the 1980s

(a) *In nominal terms*	Official Estimates (as in Table 1)	Revised Estimate
	£ billion	
Net assets at the end of 1979	+12·4	+19·5
Less the current account deficit during the 1980s	−17·2	−17·2
	−4·8	+2·3
Add the balancing item during the 1980s	+26·0	+26·0
Add the allocation of SDRs	+0·3	+0·3
	+21·5	+28·6
Add capital gains during the 1980s	+62·2	+82·3
Net assets at the end of 1989	+83·7	+110·9
Net assets at the end of 1989 at end of 1979 prices	+42·8	+56·7

(b) *In real terms*	at end-1979 prices		at end-1989 prices
	Official estimates	*Revised estimates*	*Revised estimates*
	£ billion		
Net assets at the end of 1979	+12·4	+19·5	+38·2
Net overseas investment	+11·4	+11·4	+22·3
Capital gains	+19·1	+25·8	+50·4
Assets at the end of 1989	+42·8	+56·7	+110·9

Part (b) of Table 22 (third row, final column) shows revised estimates of *real* capital gains at end-1989 prices. Over the decade of the 1980s, real capital gains amounted to £50·4 billion, an average of £5·0 billion a year. As overseas assets increased during the decade, *if* capital gains had accrued evenly over time (which they did not), then capital gains in 1989 would be running at more than £5·0 billion—at £7 billion or so a year. This figure is based on what actually happened during the 1980s; the 1990s are unlikely to be a repeat of the 1980s.

NINE

Capital Gains and the Balance of Payments

So far in this *Research Monograph* the focus of attention has been with historical-estimates of capital gains, particularly during the 1980s. In this section events during 1990 and 1991 and the prospects for capital gains in the future, which are even more difficult to estimate, are assessed.

1990 and 1991

Both 1990 and 1991 have been eventful years for overseas investment. *First*, there were substantial revisions of the estimates of the book value of UK direct investment overseas and inward investment between publication of the 1990 Pink Book and the 1991 Pink Book. The revised data have been incorporated in the earlier sections. A feature of the revisions is that net direct investment at book value at the end of 1989 was reduced from £53·1 billion to £36·2 billion, a reduction of 32 per cent, while net earnings from net direct investment in 1989 were reduced from £8 billion to £7·8 billion, a reduction of only 2½ per cent.

Second, during each of the years 1980 to 1989, direct investment overseas exceeded inward investment but for 1990 the provisional figures show inward investment of £19 billion and outward investment of £11·7 billion, reducing the net balance of UK direct overseas investment.

Third, during 1990 stock market prices in many countries fell and sterling rose, again reducing the net balance of UK overseas investment. These changes, together with the UK's current account deficit of £14·4 billion during 1990, reduced UK overseas assets from £83·7 billion at the end of 1989 to £29·6 billion at the end of 1990.

During 1991 the pattern of stock market prices and exchange rates reversed; prices on world stock markets rose and sterling fell relative to the dollar. By June 1991 the FT-Actuaries World Stock Market index excluding the UK had regained half of the fall during 1990 and the World Stock Market index excluding Japan had recovered to its end-1989 level.[1] Japanese equities have a larger weight in the World index than in UK overseas portfolio and direct investment.

As the data available for the end of 1990 are provisional and were affected by low stock market prices resulting from the Iraq Gulf crisis which was resolved in 1991, the position at the end of 1990 has been ignored. However, one aspect of the revisions to the statistics of overseas investment has had important consequences for the estimates given in Section 8. According to the *1990* Pink Book, capital losses on net direct investment between the end of 1979 and the end of 1989 were £3·6 billion. The new estimate in the *1991* Pink Book reports losses of £23·5 billion for the same period (as shown in Table 2: above, page 30), and this transformation was concentrated on 1989; capital *gains* of £12·7 billion indicated in the 1990 Pink Book were wiped out and replaced by *losses* of £0·9 billion in the 1991 Pink Book. As sterling fell sharply, by 11 per cent against the dollar and by 15 per cent against the Deutschemark in 1989, capital gains would have been expected as dollar and Deutschemark book values translated to sterling increased. Presumably this effect was more than wiped out by write-offs by companies which are treated as capital losses by the CSO. Some write-offs reflect real losses but most reflect the accounting treatment of acquisitions and reduce the book values of overseas assets used as a basis for Table 22, so the write-offs may justify some upward revision of the capital gains reported in Section 8.

Trend Capital Gains

It would be convenient to be able to estimate a trend figure for capital gains—to be able to say that, taking one year with another, capital gains will amount to, of the order of, £10 billion a year and that in 1989 they offset half the deficit of £20 billion. In practice it is possible to go part of the way, but some capital gains are dependent on the movement of particular variables which change from year to year.

Table 23 summarises the position. 'Other net liabilities' include

---

[1] FT-Actuaries World Index:

	Excluding UK	Excluding Japan	(UK)
		All in Sterling	
31 December 1989	148·01	131·91	145·91
31 December 1990	97·03	102·71	127·27
28 June 1991	123·27	130·15	143·16
9 October 1991	122·54	128·08	153·54

Table 23:
Britain's Net Overseas Assets and
Projected Capital Gains

(a)	Estimate at end-1989 £bn.	Real Capital Appreciation £bn.	% rate per year
Portfolio investment net	110[a]		
(of which equities net)	(80)[a]	3·2	4
Direct investment net	80[a]	1·6	2
Other net liabilities	−80[a]		
Total	110	4·8	

(b)	Scenarios (1)	(2) £ billion	(3)
Trend real capital gains	4·8	4·8	4·8
Scenarios			
(1) UK and world inflation at 3% a year			
(UK and world r = 7%)	0·3[b]		
	5·1		
(2) UK inflation 6%			
world inflation 3%			
UK devalues by 3%		2·7[c]	
(UK r = 10%; world = 7%)		7·5	
(3) UK inflation 6%			
world inflation 3%			
UK devalues by 0%			−3·0[d]
(UK r = 10%; world = 7%)			1·8

Notes:

[a] The estimates are rounded to the nearest £10 bn. The estimate of net portfolio investment is taken from Table 2, row 4. A multiple of 1·75 is applied to the estimate of net direct investment of £36·2 bn. shown in Table 2, row 4 and £15 bn. is added. The reasons for using a multiple of 1·75 are given in Section 8. The reasons for making a further adjustment were given at the end of the previous section. £20 bn. was added to 'Other net liabilities' for unrecorded capital inflows indicated by the balancing item.

[*Notes to Table 23 contd. on p. 90*]

bank deposits, loans from banks, other short-term assets and liabilities, and the UK foreign exchange reserves. The first column of part (a) of the Table shows Britain's net assets at the end of 1989—the estimates are the best that can be made given the uncertainties surrounding the data. Net direct investment is included at market values and it is assumed that UK borrowing is under-recorded in the official statistics—that much of the balancing item was unrecorded borrowing.

The second column of part (a) of Table 23 shows an estimate of the real capital gains on investments. The real capital gain on portfolio investment in ordinary shares is estimated at 4 per cent per year. As the *net* dividend yield was of the order of 2 per cent in 1989, that gives a total expected real return of 6 per cent and compares with the actual average annual real return of 13·5 per cent on investments in overseas equities during the 1980s by UK pension funds.[1] The estimated trend, real return on direct investment shown in Table 23 is lower than for portfolio investment because ploughed-back profits on direct investment are included as new investment. In effect it is assumed that the value of direct investment over and above the book value of that investment will continue to increase in line with portfolio investment.

Actual performance in the past suggests that UK portfolio managers will not on average out-perform world stock market indices in the long run,[2] so the return on overseas portfolio investments will match approximately movements of indices of overseas share prices.[3] Nonetheless the implied, projected, annual,

---

[1] The WM Company (1990), p. 3.   [2] The WM Company (1990), p. 33.

[3] The Japanese market accounted for almost a half of the total capitalisation of the world stock markets in 1989 and its weighting in the world index was correspondingly large. The allocation of investments to the Japanese market was an important determinant of relative performance during the 1980s.

[*Notes to Table 23 contd. from p. 89*]

[b] There are two inflation adjustments: equity investments are assumed to appreciate in line with the inflation rate and total net assets have to be adjusted for the effect of inflation to maintain the real value of net assets.

     3% on £80 bn. (portfolio investment in equities net) = £2·4 bn. + (1½%* on direct investment net of £80 bn. = £1·2 bn.) − (3% on £110 bn. = £3·3 bn.) = £0·3 bn.

* It is assumed that half the effects of faster inflation is taken as extra stock profits which are included as earnings from net direct investment.

[c] + £0·3 bn. from (b) + (devaluation adjustment: 3% of all portfolio and direct investment (£190 bn.) = £5·7 bn.) − (3% of £110 bn. = £3·3 bn.) = £2·7 bn.

[d] + £2·7 bn. from (c) − (devaluation adjustment of £5·7 bn.) = −£3·0 bn.

real return of about 7 per cent (net dividend of 2 per cent grossed up to 3 per cent plus capital appreciation of 4 per cent) is a cautious estimate of the uncertain future real return. It compares with a real yield on index-linked stocks of 4·25 per cent (as of June 1991) and indicates that investors expect a risk premium of 2·75 per cent for investing in equities. (The projected 7 per cent return compares with the actual average, annual, real, market rate of return for overseas equities during the 1980s of 16 per cent (CAPS, 1990). If this rate of return were repeated, trend real capital gains at about 12 per cent a year would be £14·4 billion, not £4·8 billion as shown in Table 23.)

Alternative Scenarios

The second part of Table 23 specifies alternative economic scenarios and their impact on capital gains. Underlying the approach is an assumption that, if the UK economy has a faster inflation rate than the world economy, then, sooner or later, it has to devalue to restore its competitiveness. (Inevitably, the scenarios are a simplified description of reality. In particular, lags are ignored; for example, overseas investors may tie-in interest yields when UK interest rates are high by acquiring longer-dated securities and may receive high rates of interest for a time after inflation and interest rates have fallen.)

If the UK and the world rate of inflation are the same, the net effect on capital gains is a small positive adjustment estimated at £0·3 billion, and the appreciation of portfolio investment in equities and direct investment would more than offset the inflation adjustment for net overseas investment. (Details of the estimates are given in note (b) to Table 23, page 90.) It should be noted that for direct investment, a proportion of the effects of inflation will be included in profits and retained profits.

If the UK has a faster rate of inflation than the rest of the world (the position of recent years) *and* devalues to offset the effects of faster inflation on competitiveness (Scenario 2), there is a substantial positive inflation adjustment of £2·7 billion, giving total capital gains of £7·5 billion. These estimates are based on estimates of net UK portfolio investment and borrowing. In addition, on balance, Britain borrows in sterling and lends in foreign currencies so there is an additional devaluation adjustment. An overall capital gains/ inflation adjustment of about £8 billion for 1989 and 1990 is indicated. This assumes that the underlying rate of inflation for the UK is about 6 per cent and that sooner or later the excess over the world rate of about 3 per cent would be offset by devaluation.

The third scenario assumes that UK inflation is faster than world inflation as in Scenario (2), but that the UK does not devalue; while such a scenario operates, the effect is to reduce capital gains, compared to the capital gains with the other scenarios in operation, but it is not sustainable in the long run—either UK inflation has to fall or sterling has to be devalued while that is still a possible option.[1]

1989

Concentration on valuations at the end of 1989 means that the estimates are to an important extent influenced by the level of stock market prices and exchange rates at 31 December 1989. Although it is very unlikely that world stock markets will continue to provide such high real returns as those obtained during the 1980s—the increases in profits relative to other components of UK national income and reductions in corporate taxes in the UK and the USA which were introduced during the 1980s are changes which boosted share prices and which cannot be repeated indefinitely; similarly, the increase in the market to book value and P/E ratios cannot continue indefinitely[2]—there are no obvious reasons for believing the UK and most overseas stock markets apart from Japan were over-valued at the end of 1989. Similarly, sterling was not in a bubble or obviously under-valued at the end of 1989. Nevertheless, there is a good deal of *uncertainty* about the trend level of stock market prices and hence the actual level of stock market prices relative to the trend level at the end of 1989. 'Fundamentals' determine share prices but only within a range, and fundamentals are themselves uncertain. ('Fundamentals' have been defined as 'the basic parameters defining an economy—such as endowments, preferences and production possibilities' (Cass, 1983). Fundamentals can be contrasted with extrinsic influences such as changes in market psychology. The fundamental value of an asset is the present value of the expected future returns from the asset.)

For 1989 and 1990, Scenario (2) provides the nearest indication of the underlying capital gains. Although that estimate is a

---

[1] These estimates of capital gains are lower than earlier estimates made by the author. A reason for the lower estimates is revisions to statistics made by the CSO.

[2] Between the end of 1979 and the end of 1989 the valuation ratio (market price to book value) of UK shares rose from 0·9 to 1·8 and the P/E ratio rose from 5·4 to 10·9. Equivalent statistics for the USA were an increase in the valuation ratio from 1·2 to 2·1 and the P/E ratio from 7·4 to 13·8. There were substantial increases in the valuation ratios for the German, French and Dutch markets. (*Source*: Morgan Stanley Capital International.)

'cautious' estimate of adjusted, trend capital gains, actual capital gains could be much higher as in 1989 and the first half of 1991, or substantial losses could be incurred as in 1990. Deviations of actual share prices from trend levels comprise three elements: temporary fluctuations about the trend caused by over-reaction to news, longer-term shifts in the trend level of share prices attributable to changing perceptions of uncertain fundamentals, and errors in estimating the trend growth of share prices.

Implications of the Capital Gains

The analysis of historical data for the 1980s (Section 8, page 86) showed *real* capital gains during the 1980s running at the average rate of £5·7 billion a year and at more than £7 billion at the end of the 1980s. The estimates of the adjusted, trend, or underlying, *nominal* capital gains given the rate of inflation suggest Britain's capital gains were of the order of £8 billion a year in 1989/90 (see page 91). It has been noted that the 1980s were particularly favourable for capital gains and that the underlying capital gains in 1989/90 were in part a reflection of the rapid inflation. Put another way, in 1989/90 high interest rates related to rapid inflation increased the charges for interest to the current account of the balance of payments; if it is assumed that sooner or later sterling would be devalued to balance the faster UK inflation, capital gains would result and provide a counter-weight to the interest charged to the current account (Scenario 2). If Britain has a faster rate of inflation than other countries and does not devalue, its balance of payments is adversely affected by interest charges (Scenario 3), but this state of affairs is likely to be temporary. In a year in which UK and world rates of inflation are 3 per cent, underlying capital gains would be of the order of £5·1 billion (Scenario 1).

Ideally, Britain would take a cautious view of the permanence of unrealised capital gains, allow its capital gains to accrue and not use them to offset a current account deficit, in the same way that a well-to-do individual may allow capital gains on his investments to accrue and build up the wealth he can leave to his children or to charity.[1] In fact, Britain's position is not so easy; there was a large deficit on the current account in 1989. In some measure Britain's position can be compared to that of an individual who would have to make sacrifices to keep his expenditure within his current income, but who has real unrealised capital gains on his

---

[1] The parallel may not apply at a macro-economic level as the existence of the capital gains could influence market operators to hold sterling assets and maintain sterling at a level which was inconsistent with a current account balance.

investments. Some economists, including A. P. Thirlwall (1992), describe the problem as the balance-of-payments 'constraint'. Their argument is that if the UK uses fiscal and/or monetary policy to boost aggregate demand and employment, the policy is self-defeating because of the ensuing deterioration in the current balance of payments as extra imports are sucked in to meet demand. In reality, the balance-of-payments constraint is a symptom of economic problems, not itself the problem. So long as Britain is tied to a fixed exchange rate, the balance-of-payments constraint can be traced to its underlying causes—relative lack of industrial entrepreneurship, an inadequately trained labour force, and inflexible wages. With more inventive and enterprising managers, a more highly qualified, skilled and experienced labour force or lower wages, the UK economy could be operated with lower unemployment at any given exchange rate. Capital gains make it possible for the UK economy to be operated at a higher level of employment and with less unemployment than would be possible in their absence because they can be set against the current balance-of-payments deficit.

There has been a presumption that Britain should aim for a zero current account balance or a surplus in the long term. Although that should, perhaps, remain an objective of policy, there is a strong case for treating capital gains as a partial offset for a deficit on the current account while policies, including policies to achieve greater flexibility of wages, are adopted to increase the long-term competitiveness of the UK economy. (It is outside the scope of this report to describe such policies; in part because the causes of differences in competitiveness are not fully understood, the design of policies to improve competitiveness is difficult.)

Liquidity

For individuals, £1 obtained by a realised capital gain is as useful as £1 of dividends or £1 received as a wage or salary. Is the same true at an international level? There are differences between exports of, say, Jaguar cars and capital gains on Britain's overseas investments. The principal difference is that the capital gains are not realised, or, if they are realised, they are often re-invested, and they are not repatriated like the proceeds of exports which are used to pay wages and buy materials and components. A deficit on the current account offset by capital gains could leave the UK with a liquidity problem. Britain has to borrow to roll over the existing short-term loans which finance part of its overseas investment; and the deficit on the current account and new net overseas investment add to this borrowing requirement. Unrealised capital gains do not offset it, but capital gains have increased Britain's net external assets, and have given the UK credibility as a borrower. In fact, Britain's net short-term financial liabilities are not large in relation to its external assets, but what is important for liquidity is that agents have very large holdings of cash and assets which they can use as security to obtain loans which they can move out of sterling.[1]

Creative Accounting

Some UK companies which grew very rapidly during the 1980s have since unravelled and creative accounting may have misled some bankers and investors in such companies. Is the exercise reported in this *Research Monograph* creative accounting on a macro-economic scale, and are there dangers in Britain's high level of overseas equity investment?

Most of the report deals with facts about the value of Britain's overseas investments; the speculative part is that which deals with projected capital gains in this section. Plainly there is uncertainty about future gains. Britain's large equity investments overseas involve risks, but so far there is no evidence that the world economy is moving into a deep recession which would undermine the value of those investments.

Summary

The summary of the UK balance-of-payments statistics given in Table 2 showed that since the liberalisation of overseas investment in 1979, the UK obtained large capital gains of £78·1 billion between the end of 1979 and the end of 1989 on its portfolio investment overseas. The statistics also indicate that net UK direct investment overseas which is valued for the official balance-of-payments statistics at book values, is under-valued. Three methods were used in Part 2 to assess the market value of UK net direct investment. It was not possible to make a precise estimate of the market value of net direct investment, but all three methods gave estimates above book value. In Section 8 the estimate of market value of net direct investment used was £27 billion above the book

---

[1] For assessing the liquidity of Britain's assets and liabilities it is noteworthy that in the official statistics both direct investment assets and liabilities have been boosted by the treatment of the Anglo-Dutch and some other companies, as described on pages 47, 48 and 49. The elimination of the contra entries would reduce direct inward investment which is included as liabilities by *proportionately* more than direct investment overseas and assets. Direct investments are among the more illiquid of assets and liabilities.

value of £36·2 billion at the end of 1989, and capital gains on net direct investment during the 1980s were estimated at £20 billion. In total, UK capital gains were £82·3 billion during the 1980s and gains on net direct investments were 24 per cent of the total.

During the 1980s capital gains more than offset deficits on the current account of the balance of payments, and they are likely to provide a substantial positive contribution to the balance of payments during the 1990s.

Notes on Estimating the Market Value of Direct Investment Overseas by the DAE Method

In this appendix details of the methods used to estimate the market value of UK direct investment overseas by the DAE method are described. The allocation of profits published by companies was used to apportion the market value of the companies. Companies use a variety of definitions of profits but before describing these definitions the treatment of loans, taxes, extraordinary items and *minority interests** should be explained.

Loans and Interest on Loans

Stock market values of the share capital of companies exclude by definition loan capital and the same consequently applies to the estimates of the value of overseas businesses based on an apportionment of share values. Investors' valuation of shares is for businesses net of their loan capital and borrowing. If a company sold its overseas businesses it would have to settle any borrowing by the overseas businesses and that would reduce the overall borrowing of the company.

Taxes

The DAE method is based on analyses of profits *before* tax because most of the regional apportionments of profits published by companies are for pre-tax profits. Investors value streams of profits and dividends *after* tax. However, tax rates in the leading industrial countries where the bulk of overseas investment is located are not very different, and so the use of before-tax profits, rather than post-tax profits, may have rather little effect; also, some important investors, including pension funds, reclaim taxes on dividends. Certain companies have been able to arrange low effective rates of tax on their published profits; it is not known whether this applies equally to overseas and UK profits.

Table A.1:
ICI's Group Profit and Loss Account

(For the year to 31 December 1989)

	1989 £m.	%
Turnover	13,171	
Operating costs	(11,884)	
Other operating income	180	
Trading profit	1,467	100
Share of profits less losses of related companies	279	19
Net interest payable	(219)	(15)
Profit on ordinary activities before taxation	1,527	104
Tax on profit on ordinary activities	(531)	(36)
Profit on ordinary activities after taxation	996	68
Attributable to minorities	(66)	(4)
Net profit attributable to parent company	930	63
Extraordinary item	127	9
Net profit for the financial year	1,057	72
Dividends	(381)	26
Profit retained for year	676	46

Source: ICI's Annual Report for 1989.

Extraordinary Items

Companies separate one-off items of expenditure and income and show them under a separate heading(s) for extraordinary or exceptional items. Although such items can have a once over effect on share prices when they are announced, if they are genuine one-off items they would not influence the value of businesses relative to their profits, and they are best ignored for the purpose of apportioning market values of companies.

Minority Interests

Ideally the interests, including share of profits, of minority shareholders in companies and their overseas businesses would be excluded when valuing overseas investment in businesses because we are concerned with the stakes owned by UK companies. In practice a regional breakdown of minority interests in profits is not provided by most companies.

The Data

The extent of the information about its overseas operations published by ICI is exceptionally comprehensive and for this reason the company's accounts are used as an example. Tables A.1 and A.2 show ICI's Profit and Loss Account and Balance Sheet for 1989, and Table A.3 the geographic breakdown of data published by ICI. The percentage breakdowns for net operating assets, turnover and trading profits earned by operations, in the UK and overseas, which are shown in Table A.3, are similar—being a little more, or a little less than 40 per cent for UK operations and close to 60 per cent for overseas operations. Net operating assets are total assets less non-operating assets, principally investments in related and other companies and less current liabilities, but before deducting loans,etc. Net operating assets are financed by share capital, reserves, loans and other creditors due after more than one year from the date of the balance sheet, and provisions. Trading profits are profits *before* inclusion of the share of profits (less losses) of related companies, and *before* deduction of net interest payable, taxes, minorities' share of profits and extraordinary items. A geographic analysis of these items apart from taxes is not published (though the international sources of ICI's loans are listed). There is an inconsistency between the definition of net assets and trading profits; net assets are calculated *after* deduction of short-term borrowings and trading profits *before* deduction of interest on short-term borrowings.

In order to obtain an approximate estimate of the value of ICI's overseas investment, the market value of ICI's share capital on 17 May 1990 when its shares were quoted at £11·43, £7,932 billion, was apportioned according to its trading profits because profits provide a more accurate indicator of the value of businesses than sales or net assets, although the latter does influence values. This gave a market value for ICI's overseas investment of £4,695 billion and it compares to the figure for net assets overseas at book value given by ICI of £4,183 billion which includes assets financed by long-term loans and provisions as well as assets financed by

Table A.2:
ICI Group Balance Sheet
(At 31 December 1989)

	1989 £ million		1989 £ million
Assets employed		**Financed by**	
Fixed assets		*Creditors due after more than one year*	
Tangible assets	4,856	Loans	1,627
Investments in related and other companies	767	Other creditors	86
	5,623		1,713
Current assets		*Provisions for liabilities and charges*	497
Stocks	2,380	Deferred income: Grants not yet credited to profit	94
Debtors	2,885	Minority interests	335
Investments and short-term deposits	250	*Capital and reserves attributable to parent company*	
Cash	133		
	5,648	Called-up share capital	694
		Reserves	
Total assets	11,271	Share premium account	384
		Revaluation reserve	56
Creditors due within one year		Other reserves	486
Short-term borrowings	(771)	Profit and loss account	3,096
Current instalments of loans	(109)	Related companies' reserves	298
Other creditors	(2,738)		
	(3,618)	Total reserves	4,320
		Total capital and reserves attributable to parent company	5,014
Net current assets	2,030		
Total assets less current liabilities	7,653		7,653

Source: ICI's Annual Report for 1989.

Table A.3:
ICI – Analysis by Geographic Region, 1989

(a) *The figures for each geographic area show the net operating assets owned by, and the turnover and profits made by companies located in that area*

	Net operating assets £m.	%	Turnover £m.	%	Trading Profit £m.	%
United Kingdom						
Sales in the UK			2,872			
Sales overseas			3,359			
	2,495	37·4	6,231	39·9	612	40·8
Continental Europe	1,026	15·4	2,928	18·8	225	15·0
The Americas	1,839	27·5	3,876	24·9	382	25·5
Asia Pacific	1,058	15·8	2,100	13·5	236	15·7
Other countries	260	3·9	451	2·9	45	3·0
	4,183	62·6	15,586	60·1	1,500	59·2
	6,678	100·0		100·0		100·0
Inter-area eliminations			(2,415)		(33)	
			13,171			
Trading profit					1,467	

(b) *Employment, turnover and geographic markets*

	Employees ('000s)[1]	Turnover £m.[2]
United Kingdom	54·7	2,917
Continental Europe	16·7	3,258
The Americas	33·9	3,867
Asia Pacific	16·7	2,378
Other countries	11·8	751
Total	133·8	13,171

[1] Average number. [2] Sales in the geographic market where customers are located.

Source: ICI's Annual Report for 1989.

shareholders' capital and reserves. (The market value of ICI's share capital can be compared with the book value of shareholders' interest in the company which is given in the penultimate row of Table A.2—£5,014 billion, giving a valuation ratio of 1·58.)

There are three main qualifications to these estimates.

o The stock market values companies on the basis of expected future profits rather than current and past profits. Plainly the use of recorded profits for the latest year to apportion stock market values is open to criticism. It can be said in support of the procedure that the latest recorded profits are an important influence on expectations and share prices and that it is the best indicator available.

o The stock market may value overseas profits differently from profits earned in the UK. The method used to apportion stock market values implicitly assumes that investors value £1 of profits earned at overseas operations the same as £1 of profits earned in the UK; on balance, if anything, they probably value overseas earnings more highly. (An advantage of profits earned overseas is that they provide a diversification from reliance on the UK economy and prospects for overseas economies may, or may not, be considered superior to those for the UK economy.) Profits arising in the USA, Europe and Japan are rated more highly than profits earned in the less developed countries, but the bulk of profits earned on Britain's overseas investments are not earned in the less developed countries. Share prices of Japanese, US and continental European companies are higher relative to dividends and *published* earnings than share prices of UK-based companies, suggesting that profits earned in these countries may be more highly rated than UK profits. If investors do value overseas profits more highly than UK profits, the method used to apportion share values under-estimates the value of overseas investment.

o ICI operates integrated businesses. If its overseas operations were sold off this would have serious consequences for the UK operations, their profitability and value.

Profits

Next, the more technical accounting qualifications are examined. There is considerable diversity of practice in defining profits for the purpose of allocation between countries or geographic areas by companies, and so an indication of the practices of other companies with overseas assets relative to the practices used by ICI is given. ICI's share price is affected by the following components of income and expenditure which are included, or excluded, as the case may be, from the geographic analysis:

o The geographic analysis of profits is made before deducting inter-area eliminations, 2·2 per cent of ICI's trading profits (see row 9 of Table A.3, page 101). ICI is almost unique in showing this as a separate item and so it is not a general problem. (Other companies presumably deduct the eliminations from country profits and give a net figure.)

o Share of profits (less losses) of related companies, which represented as much as 19 per cent of ICI's trading profits in 1989 (see row 5 of Table A.1), are excluded from the geographic analysis. (For ICI the proportion of these profits attributable to overseas rather than UK operations, was lower than for trading profits, but the exact breakdown is not available.) For 100 of the 108 companies for which a geographic breakdown of profits was used to allocate market values, it was possible to trace the treatment of the profits of related companies. Sixty-seven of the 100 companies did not receive profits from associates or included them in the area breakdown. In total, the profits of associates of the remaining 33 firms, which were not analysed by area, were equivalent to 4·4 per cent of the trading profits of the 100 companies. Some of the unallocated profits of associates will have been earned overseas but the division between overseas and domestic operations may be different from that for profits which are allocated. Ideally, all the profits of related companies would be included in the geographic analysis, but the proportion of profits affected is small, so any distortion caused by the exclusion of the profits of related companies from the geographic analysis of trading profits used for apportioning market values of companies will be limited.

o Profits attributable to minority interests (equivalent to 4 per cent of ICI's trading profits (row 10 of Table A.1)) are included in the trading profits analysed by geographic area. The percentage of profits attributable to minorities for 100 of the companies for which an apportionment of profits was used was 3·2 per cent. The percentage of overseas profits attributable to minority share-holders in overseas subsidiaries may be higher than for minority shareholders of the UK subsidiaries. Again the proportion is small.

o Net interest payable by ICI represented 15 per cent of its trading profits[1] (Table A.1, row 6). This compares with 11 per cent for the 99 companies which reported net interest payments. (ICI gave its regional allocation for profits before deduction of interest. For 10 companies the profits breakdown by geographic area was given after deducting interest—the interest payments by these 10 companies represented 0.9 per cent of the total profits allocated by the 99 companies.)

o Taxes on profits represented 36 per cent of trading profits for ICI. If tax rates differ between countries, that would affect the valuation of profits by investors (see page 97).

o The extraordinary item which was positive and represented 9 per cent of ICI's trading profits related to the disposal of a business in the USA. (The treatment of extraordinary items is discussed on page 98.)

There are many problems involved in analysing profits according to the location of operating businesses; for example, R & D expenditure and head office expenses incurred in the UK may have a bearing on profits earned in other countries. Companies do not describe in their published accounts how they make such allocations and apportionments, though a few companies explicitly exclude head office costs and/or R & D from their geographic analysis of profits. However, there is no reason to suppose that the analyses made by companies are misleading and distort the results given in the paper.

Sales
Sales are a less satisfactory basis for allocating share market values, especially for companies which trade in products subject to high indirect tax rates, because the ratio of profits to sales may vary for operations in different countries and shareholders value companies according to their expectations for profits and dividends, not sales. A further complication for some companies for which sales were used was that they allocated sales to markets and included exports as overseas sales, rather than allocated sales by the domicile of the operation from which the sales originated. The effect of this difference was to exaggerate the relative size of the overseas operations of these companies but adjustments were made to exclude estimated exports based on any relevant information given in the accounts.

---

[1] Although net interest payable and taxes on profits are given as percentages of trading profits, interest can be paid out of dividends received from associated companies and taxes are paid on profits less interest.

Table A.4:
Total Assets and UK Companies' Stakes in their Overseas Subsidiaries

	Sample of 137 companies[1] 1989	Business Monitor *(MO4, 1987)* *UK direct investment overseas 1987[2]*
		£bn.
		(Figures in brackets — total assets as a ratio of the variable)
Estimated total assets overseas	165·3	
Total assets		169·5
Stakes		
Estimated book value of companies' stakes	64·0 (2·58)	
Total		76·5 (2·2)
of which:		
Capital and reserves		59·0[3] (2·9)
Net loans and outstanding accounts due to parent		17·5

[1] The three insurance companies are excluded.

[2] Excludes banks, insurance companies and other financial institutions (*Source*: p. 35, row 3).

[3] Including minority interests. (These are excluded to make the ratio of total assets to capital stakes consistent.)

Book Value of Capital

The estimation of the book value of shareholders' interest in companies which was defined in Box 2 (above, page 46) did not present problems. The treatment used for goodwill and other intangible assets followed the practices used by companies; some companies included intangible assets as assets, while many had written them off against reserves or set them against their share capital and reserves in their balance sheets.

Although ICI publishes a geographic analysis of the employment of its net operating assets (Table A.3, column 1), most companies do not include this information in their published accounts. An estimate of the book value of the net assets employed at overseas subsidiaries is required to relate the aggregate market value of companies' investments overseas to the estimates of the book values of assets included in official published statistics. In Section 4 and in this Appendix the book value of net assets employed overseas is obtained by apportioning the total net assets of companies in the same way as market values are apportioned.

A Check on the Consistency of the Estimates

Table A.4 relates the estimated book value of total assets overseas for the sample companies to the *estimated* book value of the companies' stakes in their overseas businesses (both total assets and book value of stakes were estimated by apportionment based on profits, etc). The ratio, 2·58, for the sample of companies can be compared with the same relationship for the population of companies from which the CSO collected data for 1987. When net loans and outstanding accounts were included in companies' stakes the ratio for this population was 2·2 and when they were excluded and total assets were related to capital and reserves alone the ratio was 2·85 (*Source: Business Monitor*, MO4, 1987). It is noteworthy that the ratio for the DAE sample of companies, 2·58, lies approximately midway between the two ratios calculated from the census data. This comparison suggests that the procedure used to estimate book values of companies' stakes under-estimates total stakes, as would be expected because a part of the net outstanding accounts is trade credit rather than capital. A qualification to these comparisons is that the DAE sample data are for 1989 and the CSO data are for 1987.

The American Method – Data Requirements and Problems

In order to apply the method used by the Bank of England the following data are required:

Inward Investment

1. The initial stock of inward investment in a base year.

2. Annual investment flows to the UK.

3. Revaluations of inward investments.

4. For 1 to 3 stocks, flows and revaluations should distinguish equity capital and amounts owing to parent companies.

5. Indices of UK share prices.

6. Data to adjust stock market indices for ploughed-back profits.

7. The ratio of market to book value of investment in the base year.

Outward Investment

For outward investment the same data are required, but for each country in which UK direct investment is located, and in addition exchange rates are used to convert data in overseas currencies to sterling.

Data Problems

Comprehensive data for aggregate inward and outward investment are available only since 1984. Prior to 1984 information to divide flows of investment in the oil industry between increases in share capital and reserves and amounts owed to parent companies is not available. For the period prior to 1984 estimates of revaluations are not available. During the period 1978 to 1984 the coverage of the statistics was increased to include insurance companies and banks.

For outward investment data problems are much more serious than for inward investment. Even when the analysis is limited to the main countries which are host to UK investment the problems include:

(a) No information on revaluations by countries is published, so revaluations can be estimated only by a process of elimination.

(b) The need to preserve confidentiality results in gaps in the statistics for share capital and reserves and amounts owed to parent companies; for example, for the Netherlands in 1987 (*Business Monitor*, MO4, 1987).

(c) Direct investment in financial institutions is not separated into share capital and reserves and amounts owed to parents (*Business Monitor*, MO4, 1987).

Estimates of the Value of Direct Investment for the USA

The summary of estimates of the value of US direct investment in other countries and inward investment to the USA given in Table C.1 and the comments given below upon the estimates, were prepared by the US Bureau of Economic Analysis. The important point to note is that the revaluation of US overseas investment to the USA in terms of stock market values is twice, or more, the book value, while the multiple for inward investment is much less. One explanation for the low multiple for inward investment is that much of the investment has taken place in recent years. (The book value of inward investment increased by 383 per cent between 1980 and 1989 compared with an increase of only 73 per cent for the book value of US outward investment.) Also, share prices on the US stock markets rose relatively slowly compared with some other stock markets during the 1980s.

For Britain the growth of the stock of outward and inward investment has been more even, though the growth of the stock of outward investment has exceeded that for inward investment, the reverse of the American position—inward investment increased by 228 per cent between 1980 and 1989 and outward investment by 320 per cent at book values. The relatively slow appreciation of US stock market prices during the 1980s which damped down the appreciation of inward investment in the USA, had an adverse effect on the market value of UK net direct investment overseas.

The methodologies used to prepare the estimates listed in Table C.1 are:

Eisner and Pieper—Market Values

The estimates are based on movements of index numbers of share prices since 1950 in host countries for direct investment. *The series of index numbers are adjusted to exclude the effects of ploughed-back profits*—that is, retained earnings are taken out of the indices. A feature of the estimates of outward investment to which the authors draw attention is that investment in Asia including Japan

Table C.1:
Estimates of US Direct Investment

Sources:	Valuation	US Direct Investment Abroad	Foreign Direct Investment in the USA	Net
		(Billions of dollars)		
		(Figures in brackets are ratios of book values)		
Eisner and Pieper (1991) for 1989	book value	373	400	−2
Eisner and Pieper (1991) for 1989	(market value)	889 (2·4)	544 (1·4)	360
	(replacement value)	801 (2·1)	453 (1·1)	409
Ulan and Dewald (1989) for 1987	(market value)	1016 (3·1)	496 (1·5)	521
	(capitalised earnings)	808 (2·5)	162 (0·5)	646
Lederer (1990) for 1988	(replacement value for property, plant and equipment; and inventory)	407 (1·2)	329 (1·0)	78
Landefeld and Lawson in *Survey of Current Business* for May 1989	(market value)	805	544	261
	(current cost, replacement value)	536	458	78

accounted for only 11 per cent of outward direct investment at book values, but 42 per cent of the excess of market over book values at the end of 1989 and 58 per cent of the revaluation of net investment (outward *less* inward investment). The extent to which the use of the Japanese stock market indices accurately reflects changes in the value of IBM and other US companies' investments in Japan must be an open question.

Eisner and Pieper—Replacement Value

To calculate replacement value Eisner and Pieper substitute investment-goods price indices (usually the fixed-investment implicit-price deflator) for host countries for stock market indices. It is assumed that the value of total direct investments including investments in intangible assets move in line with price indices for investment goods. As noted on page 26 (note 1), there is an important qualification to this method because some inflation gains are treated as profits and the method results in double-counting. (As the authors acknowledge, much more goes into the value of an investment than fixed assets.)

Ulan and Dewald—Market Value

Ulan and Dewald also used indices of share prices to calculate market values but they did not adjust the share indices for ploughed-back profits and this explains the higher market values which they estimate compared with those given by Eisner and Pieper, whose methodology is the correct one. It is noteworthy that Eisner and Pieper's estimates of market values for 1987 are nearly 40 per cent lower than Ulan and Dewald's estimates.

Ulan and Dewald—Capitalised Earnings

Earnings were divided by the P/E ratio for the S & P 500 stocks to calculate capitalised earnings.

Lederer—Replacement Value

Lederer limited the use of replacement values to fixed assets and inventories. He did not use price indices for investment goods to revalue total investments from the time the investments were made—the Eisner and Pieper revaluation method. He revalued assets held at the end of each period in terms of their replacement cost at that point in time. Another methodological difference was that Lederer used the ratio of current to historical cost for US non-financial businesses to revalue assets in the USA *and* in foreign countries.

Landefeld and Lawson (L & L)—Market Value

The methodology used by L & L was the same as that used by Eisner and Pieper except that:

(a) L & L use indices of share prices to revalue flows of equity capital, not total direct investment flows—increases in the net amounts owed to parents are excluded.

(b) L & L revalue investment from the end of 1966 and in order to get an initial estimate of market values at that time they used:

   (i) the ratio of market value to book value for the Standard and Poor's Index for inward investment;

   (ii) grossed-up dividends for outward investment.

Table C.2:
A Comparison of the Location of US and UK Direct Investment in 1987

(At Book Value)

Location	UK		USA		Ratio of Market Value to Book Value[a]
	£bn.	(%)	$bn.	(%)	
Total	86·7[a]		308·0[a]		2·0
Canada	5·2	(6·0)	58·4	(19·0)	1·3
USA	30·6	(35·3)	–		1·1[c]
UK	–		42·0	(13·6)	1·8
Germany	3·4	(3·9)	24·8	(8·1)	1·4
France	3·0	(3·5)	11·8	(3·8)	1·8
Netherlands	11·5	(13·3)	14·4	(4·7)	1·2
Japan	0·9	(1·0)	14·7	(4·8)	7·0
Australia	6·0	(6·9)	11·1	(3·6)	1·2
Other	26·1	(30·1)	130·8	(42·5)	2·1

[a] Including amounts owed to parent companies.
[b] Based on the use of stock market indices.
[c] Includes all inward investment not UK investment in the USA alone.
Sources: Eisner and Pieper (1991) and *Business Monitor*, MO4, 1987.

For inward investment L & L's estimate is identical to that obtained by Eisner and Pieper.

Landefeld and Lawson—Current Cost

L & L followed the methodology used by Lederer—the revaluation was applied to tangible assets only.

Location of Direct Investment

The location of US and UK foreign direct investment is compared in Table C.2. The USA is, of course, a much more important host for UK investment than vice versa. For the UK the Netherlands is important because of the treatment of the Anglo Dutch companies.

Overall the ratio of market value to book value for US foreign investment is 2·0. When the same ratios for countries were related to the pattern of UK overseas investment, the overall ratio was 1·5. (The US ratios do not necessarily apply to UK investment because

Table C.3:
US Direct Investment, 1950-1989

| | Outward Direct Investment | | | | Inward Direct Investment | | | |
| | Book Value | Market Value based on share prices | Ratio | Replacement Value | Book Value | Market Value | Ratio | Replacement Value |
		$ billion				$ billion		
1950	11·8	11·8 [a]	1·0	11·8 [b]	3·4	3·4	1·0	3·4
1955	19·4	29·7	1·53	22·2	5·1	8·5	1·7	5·3
1960	31·9	51·3	1·61	39·3	6·9	11·1	1·6	6·9
1965	49·5	81·2	1·64	61·3	8·8	17·9	2·0	9·0
1970	75·5	108·3	1·44	108·6	13·3	19·6	1·5	14·0
1975	124·1	149·2	1·20	263·0	27·7	27·0	1·0	29·8
1980	215·4	295·2	1·37	533·4	83·0	75·0	0·9	77·9
1985	229·7	403·6	1·76	54·7	184·6	209·8	1·1	185·6
1989	373·4	888·6	2·38	800·7	400·8	544·1	1·4	412·9

[a] Market values were assumed to equal book values in 1950.
[b] Replacement values were assumed to equal book values in 1950.

Source: Eisner & Pieper, 'The World's Greatest Debtor Nation?', Updated and Revised Tables (25 January 1991).

the timing of investments was different.) One explanation for the lower ratio for the UK is that it has less investment in Japan. Also the ratio used for the UK's large investment in the USA is only 1·1; the average for all inward investment is used, but the ratio for UK investment in the USA may be higher because on average it is older and because of the write-downs of UK investment in the USA.

Finally, Table C.3 records the growth of US direct investment since 1950 at book value, market value and replacement value.

Glossary

Balancing Item: As with any other double-entry book-keeping system, the balance-of-payments accounts should balance. In fact they do not because of errors. A balancing item is included each year to bring the sum of all balance-of-payments entries for the year to zero, reflecting both persistent elements, where certain types of transactions are not adequately covered in the accounts, and erratic fluctuations which are likely to be, in part, timing errors in the recording of transactions and the corresponding payments.

Book Value of Assets and Liabilities: See Box 2, pp. 46-47.

Capital Gains: Realised capital gains are increases in the value of a capital asset when it is sold or transferred, compared with its initial worth. Unrealised capital gains are increases in the market value of an asset which is held over its initial worth. Inflation and currency movements can result in capital gains. Real capital gains are gains over and above changes in the value of assets which reflect changes in the general price level which is usually measured by the retail price index.

Capital Transactions: Capital transfers, transactions in UK external assets and liabilities, Exchange Equalisation Account (EEA) losses on forward commitments, allocation of Special Drawing Rights (SDRs) and gold subscription to the IMF. The main capital transactions relate to the short- and longer-term transactions in UK external assets and liabilities.

Current Account of the Balance of Payments: That part of the balance-of-payments accounts recording current, i.e. non-capital, transactions, comprising visible trade, services, interest, profits and dividends, and non-capital transfers.

Creative Accounting: The manipulation of financial reports so as to mislead some users of accounts about the true state of a company's affairs without this constituting fraudulent reporting.

Depreciation: The reduction in value of an asset through wear and tear. An allowance for the depreciation on a company's assets is always made before the calculation of profit on the grounds that the consumption of capital assets is one of the costs of earning the revenues of the business.

Direct Investment: Outward investment by companies is investment by UK companies in their overseas subsidiaries, branches, or associated companies. Inward direct investment is investment by companies resident overseas in their UK subsidiaries, branches and associate companies. A direct investment in a company means that the investor has a significant influence on the operations of the company. Investment covers acquisition of fixed assets, stockbuilding, stock appreciation, and all other financial transactions, such as additions to working capital and acquisitions of securities.

Earnings: Earnings are the profits of companies. Most companies distribute a part of their profits as dividends and plough-back (retain) the balance.

Equities—Ordinary Shares: The risk capital of a company. Investors in equity shares are not guaranteed to get either a dividend or their money back, but they do get the chance of income and capital growth. Owners have the right to vote in company affairs usually in proportion to the number of shares they hold, but receive a dividend only after bondholders and other classes of shareholder have been paid the amounts due to them.

FIFO (First in First Out): The term relates to the method of valuing stocks, whether it is assumed that the first, earliest batch of goods received is the first to be dispatched or used for production, FIFO, or whether the last or latest batch of goods received is the first out, LIFO.

Gross: See NET.

Historical Cost Accounting: Under the historical cost accounting convention transactions and assets are recorded at the prices ruling when transactions occur or the assets were acquired. Assets, liabilities and profits are not adjusted to distinguish the effects of changes in the general level of prices.

LIFO (Last in First Out): See FIFO.

Minority Interests: Equity interests in a subsidiary company which are held by owners other than the controlling parent company.

Net: The term net is frequently used in the paper for the difference

116

between outward and inward investment or for net overseas assets—assets located overseas owned by UK residents less assets in the UK owned by residents of other countries. The term gross signifies the outward investment or overseas assets owned by UK residents before offsetting inward investment or assets in the UK owned by residents of other countries.

Nominal Values: Nominal values are values at contemporary prices and are distinguished from real values which are values adjusted for changes in the general level of prices since a base date. *See* REAL VALUES.

Ordinary Shares: See EQUITIES.

Permanent Income: The expected trend level of income of a consumer. The idea is that consumers smooth out expected fluctuations in their income when deciding upon their expenditure.

Ploughed-back (Retained) Profits: Profits which are not distributed as dividends but which are re-invested in the company.

Portfolio Investment: Overseas portfolio investment is investment in securities issued by overseas registered companies, other than direct investment, and in securities issued by overseas governments to UK residents. Securities covered are those having an original contractual maturity of more than one year and those with no fixed maturity. A portfolio investment does not entitle the investor to any significant influence over the operations of the company or institution. Inward portfolio investment is investment in UK registered companies by persons resident overseas.

Real Values: When changes in values over a period of time are considered it is often useful to make the comparison in terms of constant prices. The percentage change in the nominal values of assets and liabilities is adjusted for the change in retail or consumer prices between the two dates so that comparisons are made relative to movements in these price indices—the adjusted changes in values are changes in 'real' values.

Revaluations: Revaluations are changes in the values of assets and are attributable to a number of causes. Assets and liabilities located overseas, when valued in sterling, change in value with changes in exchange rates between sterling and the currencies of countries in which the assets or liabilities are located. Changes in the general level of prices are another explanation for revaluations; at intervals many companies revalue their properties which very

117

approximately increase in value in line with general inflation. Companies, particularly UK companies, which acquire—takeover—companies at values in excess of the values placed on the tangible and monetary assets often write-off the excess and these write-offs are treated as revaluations.

SDRs (Special Drawing Rights): Reserve assets created and distributed by decision of the members of the International Monetary Fund (IMF). Participants accept an obligation to provide convertible currency to another participant in exchange for SDRs equivalent to three times their own allocation. Only countries with a sufficiently strong balance of payments are designated by the IMF to do so. SDRs may also be used in certain direct payments between participants, and for payments of various kinds to the IMF.

Stakes: Stakes are the interests of companies in their subsidiaries. They can be measured at book or market values. If a holding company owns all of the shares issued by a subsidiary, the company's stake is measured by the total value of the company. Where there are minority interests these have to be deducted. Stakes comprise the share capital owned by the holding company and any loans and outstanding accounts owed to it by the subsidiary. (*See* Box 2, pp. 46-47.)

Stock Market Indices: Stock market indices measure movements of stock market prices. They are weighted averages of share prices on a series of dates as percentages of prices on a base date. The coverage of quoted shares by the indices varies.

Subsidiaries: Companies legally controlled by other companies. A company is a subsidiary when between 50 and 100 per cent of its shares are owned by another company or another company owns less than 50 per cent of its shares but controls its management.

Valuation Ratio: The valuation ratio for a share is the ratio of the market value to book value of the share shown in the company's latest published accounts.

Bibliography/References

Balasubramanyan, V. N., and D. T. Nguyen (1990): 'International Dimensions of the Food and Drink Processing Industries', Lancaster University.

Bank of England Quarterly Bulletin (1990): 'The external balance sheet of the United Kingdom: recent developments and measurement problems', *Bank of England Quarterly Bulletin*, Vol. 30, No. 4, November, pp. 487-99.

Blanchard, O. J., and S. Fischer (1989): *Lectures on Macroeconomics*, Cambridge, Mass.: MIT Press.

Branson, W. H., and D. W. Henderson (1985): 'Specification and Influence of Asset Markets', in R. N. Jones and P. B. Kenen (eds.), *Handbook of International Economics*, Vol. II, Amsterdam: Elsevier.

Business Statistics Office (1990): *Business Monitor MO4*, London: HMSO.

CAPS, General Report 1989 (1990): *Pension Fund Investment Performance*, Leeds: Combined Actuarial Performance Services Ltd.

Cass, D., and K. Shell (1983): 'Do Sunspots Matter?', *Journal of Political Economy*, Vol. 91, No. 2, April, pp. 193-227.

Casson, M. (1990): 'International Transmission of Macroeconomic Disturbances: The Role of Equity Markets', New York: Columbia University, Department of Economics Discussion Paper Series, No. 466.

Central Statistical Office (1990): 'Census of overseas assets 1987', *Business Monitor MO4*, London: HMSO.

Central Statistical Office (1990): 'The Pink Book 1990: United Kingdom Balance of Payments', London: HMSO.

Central Statistical Office (1991): 'Overseas Direct Investment (1989)', London: HMSO.

Cohen, B. J. (1969): *Balance of Payments Policy*, Harmondsworth: Penguin.

Coutts, K., and W. Godley (1990): 'Prosperity and Foreign Trade in the 1990s', *Oxford Review of Economic Policy*, Vol. 6, No. 3.

Dornbusch, R. (1988): *Exchange Rates and Inflation*, Cambridge, Mass.: MIT Press.

Eisner, R., and P. J. Pieper (1991): 'Real Foreign Investment in Perspective', *Annals of The American Academy of Political and Social Sciences*, Vol. 516, July, pp. 22-35.

Eisner, R., and P. J. Pieper (1990): 'The World's Greatest Debtor Nation?', *The North American Review of Economics and Finance*, Vol. 1, No. 1, pp. 9-32.

Gavin, M. (1989): 'The stock market and exchange rate dynamics', *Journal of International Money and Finance*, Vol. 8, No. 2, June, pp. 181-200.

Gavin, M. (1990): 'International Transmission of Macroeconomic Disturbances: The Role of Equity Markets', New York: Columbia University, Discussion Paper Series No. 466.

Gavin, M. (1991): 'Animal Spirits, Terms of Trade and the Current Account: The Role of Financial Market Integration', New York: Columbia University, Discussion Paper Series No. 527.

Hicks, J. R. (1939): *Value and Capital*, Oxford: Oxford University Press.

Krugman, P. R. (1989): *Exchange-Rate Instability*, Cambridge, Mass.: The MIT Press.

Landefeld, J. S., M. Mann, and H. Townsend (1990): 'Valuation of the Stocks of US and Foreign Direct Investment', Bureau of Economic Analysis, US Dept. of Commerce, Discussion Paper 49.

Landefeld, J. S., and A. M. Lawson (1991): 'Valuation of the US Net International Investment Position', *Survey of Current Business*, Vol. 71, No. 5, May, pp. 40-49.

Lederer, W. (1990): 'The Valuation of US Direct Investments Abroad', Washington DC: Board of Governors of the Federal Reserve System.

Lederer, W. (1990): 'Problems in Defining and Estimating the Market Values of International Direct Investment Positions', Washington DC: Board of Governors of the Federal Reserve System.

Reddaway, W. B. (1968): *Effects of UK Direct Investment Overseas: Final Report*, Cambridge: Cambridge University Press.

Scholl, R. B. (1990): 'International Investment Position: Component Detail for 1989', *Survey of Current Business*, Vol. 70, No. 6, pp. 54-65.

Shleifer, A., and L. H. Summers (1990): 'The Noise Trader Approach to Finance', *Journal of Economic Perspectives*, Vol. 4, No. 2, pp. 19-33.

Skeoch, K., and Gwyn Hacche (1990): Keynotes 'Amber Light for Rates', James Capel & Co. Ltd., circular.

Silberston, A., D. Shepherd, and R. Strange (1985): *British Manufacturing Investment Overseas*, London: Methuen.

Spanneut, C. (1990): 'Direct Investment of the European Economy', *Report to Eurostat*, Luxembourg.

Steuer, M. D. *et al.* (1973): *The impact of foreign direct investment on the United Kingdom*, London: HMSO.

Stone, R., and G. Stone (1964): *National Income and Expenditure*, London: Bowes & Bowes.

Thirlwall, A. P., and H. D. Gibson (1992): *Balance-of-Payments Theory and the United Kingdom Experience*, London: Macmillan.

Ulan, M., and W. G. Dewald (1989): 'The U.S. Net International Investment Position: Mistaken and Misunderstood', in J. A. Dorn and W. A. Niskanen (eds.), *Dollars, Deficits and Trade*, Boston, Mass.: Kluwer.

United Nations Centre on Transnational Corporations (1988): *Transnational Corporations in World Development—Trends and Prospects*, New York and London: HMSO.

Weale, M. *et al.* (1989): *Macroeconomic Policy*, London: Unwin Hyman.

Winters, L. Alan (1985): *International Economics*, London: George Allen & Unwin.

Whittington, G. (1990): *The Valuation Basis of Financial Reporting*, Cambridge: Cambridge University Press.

WM Company (1990): *WM UK Pension Fund Service Annual Review 1989*, Edinburgh: The World Markets Co. Plc.

Competition or Credit Controls?

DAVID T. LLEWELLYN and MARK HOLMES

The 1980s experienced one of the fastest growth rates of lending to the personal sector of any decade this century. Personal sector debt rose by around £350 billion and lending to the personal sector expanded at an average annual rate of 19 per cent. The decade was also a period of major deregulation, structural change, and enhanced competition in the financial system. Although inflation was reduced sharply early in the decade, it accelerated in the later years. One of the factors identified by the Bank of England as contributing to the latter acceleration was 'a massive increase in the availability of credit, whose roots can be traced back to the lifting of a series of restrictions on lending institutions in the early 1980s'.

This relaxation of controls over the financial system is central to understanding both why there was the surge in credit and whether controls would be effective in the future. Easing regulation made the financial system more competitive as different sectors of the market were no longer segregated from each other.

This increase in competition had its customary effect, lowering prices and widening the range of financial services available. Not surprisingly, demand surged especially from the tightly restricted personal sector. This surge in demand was channelled primarily through the housing market causing a disequilibrium or stock-adjustment process.

In this *Hobart Paper*, David Llewellyn and Mark Holmes argue that such a process of stock adjustment is likely to be insensitive to price but that, once it is over, the rate of growth of credit from its new level would once again be controllable by price (i.e. interest rates). Market conditions which have revived interest in credit controls among politicians, journalists and academics, were temporary and have now disappeared.

Hobart Paper 117

ISBN 0-255 36300-1

£7.95

The Institute of Economic Affairs
2 Lord North Street, Westminster
London SW1P 3LB
Telephone: 071-799 3745

Monetarism and Monetary Policy

ANNA J. SCHWARTZ

The emergence of monetarism as an alternative to orthodox Keynesian theory owes much to the pioneering work of Anna J. Schwartz. *A Monetary History of the United States, 1867-1960*, which she co-authored with Milton Friedman, has become a classic, and has changed the way in which economists study monetary policy and monetary history.

In this *Occasional Paper*, she examines the transformation from pegged to floating exchange rates, and assesses the behaviour of these rates in relation to monetary policy. Are they an appropriate objective of policy? Do they provide information about monetary conditions?

The sale or purchase of foreign currency by the monetary authorities has no demonstrable effect on the exchange market, apart from adding to the uncertainty of those who play the market, but it can distort domestic monetary growth and ultimately the price level.

Although the conclusions reached are largely, but not exclusively, based on her studies of the United States, they do have important policy implications for Britain and other countries. Monetary policy can stabilise the exchange rate *or* the price level – but not both.

Occasional Paper 86

ISBN 0-255 36302-8

The Institute of Economic Affairs
2 Lord North Street, Westminster
London SW1P 3LB
Telephone: 071-799 3745

£3.95